GOR

D1486026

WHERE WE ARE

WHERE WE ARE

The State of Britain Now

Roger Scruton

BLOOMSBURY

LONDON · OXFORD · NEW YORK · NEW DELHI · SYDNEY

Bloomsbury Continuum
An imprint of Bloomsbury Publishing Plc

50 Bedford Square   1385 Broadway
London   New York
WC1B 3DP   NY 10018
UK   USA

www.bloomsbury.com

BLOOMSBURY, CONTINUUM and the Diana logo are trademarks of
Bloomsbury Publishing Plc

First published 2017

British Library Cataloguing-in-Publication Data
A catalogue record for this book is available from the British Library.

Library of Congress Cataloguing-in-Publication data has been applied for.

ISBN: HB: 978-1-4729-4788-8
      EPDF: 978-1-4729-4786-4
      EPUB: 978-1-4729-4787-1

2 4 6 8 10 9 7 5 3 1

Typeset by Newgen KnowledgeWorks Pvt. Ltd., Chennai, India
Printed and bound in Great Britain by CPI Group (UK) Ltd, Croydon CR0 4YY

To find out more about our authors and books visit www.bloomsbury.com.
Here you will find extracts, author interviews, details of forthcoming
events and the option to sign up for our newsletters.

Was du ererbt von deinen Vätern hast,
Erwirb es, um es zu besitzen.

(What you have inherited from your ancestors,
Earn it, so as to own it.)

Goethe, *Faust*

CONTENTS

CONTENTS

PREFACE

The European treaties have imposed laws on our country without discussion in Parliament, while Parliament has referred two vitally important matters – the unity of the Kingdom and our membership of the European Union – to the people, asking them (though in the first case only some of them) to choose by referendum what our future should be. Does this mean that the United Kingdom is no longer a representative democracy? It is surely clear that legislation issuing from a Treaty, of which we are only one among 28 signatories, is not legislation issuing uniquely from our elected representatives, and that decisions made through plebiscite are not decisions of Parliament. How, in these circumstances, do we define our identity as a body politic, and what in the coming years will hold us together, as a single people subject to a single rule of law? This book sets out to answer those questions, and to understand the volatile moment in which we live.

Previous drafts were read by Tim Congdon, Mark Dooley, Alicja Gescinska, Maurice Glasman, Bob Grant, Douglas Murray and Robert Tombs, and I have benefited greatly from their advice.

Malmesbury, June 2017

PRELUDE

This short book is a personal response to the 'Brexit' decision, but not an argument for it. Whether or not the British people were right to vote as they did, they are now committed to leaving the European Union, and the question that I address is how our national sovereignty should be conceived in order to bring the 'leavers' and the 'remainers' together.

Some will say that the British people are not committed to leaving the European Union since, in our system of representative government, binding decisions are taken by the Queen in Parliament, and not directly by the people. And they might point to the subsequent general election, in which Theresa May, having made Brexit central to her platform, lost her majority, as though the referendum were now of dwindling significance, and outside the real business of Parliament. On the other hand, it was a decision of Parliament to seek a popular vote, and it was assumed on every side that the question lay beyond the reach of normal government, being an issue about our identity as a political community.

In fact, the British people used the referendum to express feelings that had been largely excluded from the political process. David Cameron did not at first perceive this, but, waking up to the reality of popular sentiment and attempting to secure the result on which he had staked his career, he warned of the economic catastrophe that awaits us, should we withdraw from the single market. And he produced one expert after another to prove the point.

Not all the voters, however, were persuaded. The experts had a point; but they sounded like people who could settle anywhere and always be on top of things. For such people it is no great imposition to be governed from elsewhere. Elsewhere is where they always are. For many ordinary voters, however, whose networks are also neighbourhoods, the issue of who governs us, and from where, is real and urgent. For such people something was at stake that had been systematically overlooked by the politicians, and which was more important to them than all the economic and geopolitical arguments, namely the question of identity: who are we, where are we, and what holds us together in a shared political order? It is not only the British who are faced with this question: it is the political question of our time, and all across Europe people are beginning to ask it. Moreover, it is not a question that can be settled by economic arguments, since it must be answered before any economic arguments make sense.

Identities are many, and often compete with each other. I have an identity as a writer, as a philosopher, as a husband and a father. In the various spheres in which I live and act, I recognize constraints, norms, duties and freedoms that belong to those spheres and provide them with their meaning. In that sense an identity assigns me to a group. But some groups also *act* as groups, taking decisions on behalf of their members and requiring the members to accept what is undertaken in their name. Hence when we act collectively – as in a committee, a team or a club – we need a clear conception of who belongs with us, and why. This conception will define what the members owe to each other and why they are included in the deal. It will be the foundation of the trust on which the collective is built. It is in this sense that politics presupposes a shared identity: a definition of who is included that enables each of us to adopt the decisions made in our name.

But what happens when trust disintegrates? In particular, what happens when the issues closest to people's hearts are neither discussed nor mentioned by their representatives, and when these issues are precisely issues of identity – of who we are, who is included and who is not? This, it seems to me, is where we have got to in Western democracies – in the United States just as much as in Europe. And recent events on both continents would be less surprising if the media and the politicians had woken up earlier to the fact that Western democracies – all of them without exception – are suffering from a crisis of identity. The 'we' that is the foundation of trust and the *sine qua non* of representative government has been jeopardized not only by the global economy and the rapid decline of indigenous ways of life, but also by the mass immigration of people with other languages, other customs, other religions, and other and competing loyalties. Worse than this is the fact that we cannot question this publicly without risking the charge of 'racism and xenophobia', and therefore cannot begin the process of coming to terms with it by discussing what the costs and benefits might be.

That is one reason why people no longer trust the political class. The Brexit referendum in Britain, the elections of Donald Trump and Emmanuel Macron, the rise of 'outsider' political parties in France, Germany, the Netherlands, Italy, Spain, Sweden, Greece and Finland – all these unforeseen developments point to a breakdown in trust between the electorate and the political establishment. And the reason for this is everywhere the same, namely that politicians have failed to stand up for the nation, or to affirm what many of its members see as their inherited rights.

The question of identity is bound up with that of sovereignty: who governs us, and from where? The European

4

Union has evolved rapidly, and through a process of institution-building, so that the question of sovereignty has often been difficult to answer. It began with the Treaty of Paris of 1951, establishing the 'European Coal and Steel Community' (ECSC). This was designed to place coal and steel – then the principal resources of military power – outside the monopoly control of any national government. But the intention was not merely to create obstacles in the path of a third European war. The intention of the founders, and of Jean Monnet in particular, was to create a union of states, which would pool their sovereignty in a shared form of government. By a separate Treaty, the Treaty of Rome of 1957, the members of the ECSC set up the European Economic Community and the European Atomic Energy Commission, the first of which was to be a 'customs union' running a common market for goods, services and labour, and a Common Agricultural Policy. A Merger Treaty of 1967 combined the three institutions, and the resulting European Community incorporated a succession of new members, leading to a revision of the Treaty of Rome and the eventual creation, via the Maastricht Treaty of 1992, of the European Union as we know it today.

An elaborate and ingenious set of institutions was devised for the administration of this supranational entity, together with an activist Court of Justice empowered to interpret all laws passed under the

Treaties in the interest of the ultimate goal of political union. The result has been a legislative inheritance – the *acquis communautaire* – that now runs to 180,000 pages, and which overrides any conflicting decision of a national parliament.

The hope of the more radical federalists, such as Jacques Delors, Jean-Claude Juncker and Guy Verhofstadt, has been to create a democratic superstate, with the European Parliament as its legislative assembly, and the European Commission as the locus of executive power. But, although these institutions have removed sovereignty from the member states, they have not really acquired it for themselves. The pooling of sovereignty has fuelled emergencies in Greece and Italy. But they are national emergencies, and the European Commission has no power to address them. The polyglot Parliament can discuss what to do. But discussion is generally as far as it goes, and in all serious matters the legislative initiative remains with the European Commission. Moreover, the Parliament is too diverse, too detached from the many national interests for people to consider that it really represents them, a fact revealed in the low turnout (around 43 per cent) in European elections. Hence the Greeks, in the emergency created by their adoption of the euro, turn to their national Parliament for a solution, only to find that it has lost control of the matter, without passing control to anyone else.[1]

In a democracy it is the people who confer power on their government, and it is to the people that the government is answerable. That is why the questions of sovereignty and identity are connected: we need to know who the people are, where they are, and what holds them together. There can be no democracy without a *demos*, a 'we', united by a shared sense of belonging. The definition of this 'we' is my theme in what follows. Although my concern is with Britain, my approach could be applied equally to France, Italy or the Czech Republic (to mention only those countries to which I am emotionally attached). On the other hand, it is impossible to consider identity, as I understand it, without roaming through a field of historical and cultural contingencies. Necessarily I shall be discussing specific things that we, the British, have to rely upon in forging a future for ourselves, and if I occasionally look across the Channel, it will be to remind the reader that the question of identity is a question for all thinking Europeans, and is not going to go away.

The European Commission warns repeatedly against the 'populism' and 'nationalism' that threaten the

---

[1] See the illuminating, if somewhat egotistical, account by Greek Finance Minister Yanis Varoufakis, *Adults in the Room: My Battle with Europe's Deep Establishment*, London, 2017.

equilibrium of Europe, suggesting that even to raise the question of national identity is to take a step away from civilization. And it is true that there are dangers here, some of which I discuss in what follows. However, it is worth pointing out that we in the Anglosphere have a language in which to discuss nationality that is not tainted by bellicose slogans – a language with a respectable past and an acknowledged political use. When we wish to summon the 'we' of political identity we refer to our *country*. We do not use grand and tainted honorifics such as *la patrie* or *das Vaterland*. We refer simply to this spot of earth, which belongs to us because we belong to it, have loved it, lived in it, defended it, and established peace and prosperity within its borders.

Moreover, as I hope to show, there is something specific about the British identity that is not present in quite the same way in other European nations. This specific thing is accountability – a feature of our lifestyle and our government that runs through all things, and which is at the origin of the British reluctance to be governed by those whose attachments lie elsewhere. This accountability is not an abstract or merely legal thing. It is a feature of the country itself. Accountability, as the British people understand and respond to it, originates in no particular person, no particular office, no particular procedure or institution: it grows in the place where we are.

OUR COUNTRY: RIGHT OR LEFT

When Britain faced the prospect of annihilation from Hitler's armies, George Orwell wrote a famous essay – *The Lion and the Unicorn* – urging his readers to unite in defence of their country.[1] The ability of the British to defend themselves, he argued, had been undermined from within, by both right and left. The bewildered remnant of the old ruling class, and the left-wing intellectuals who recoiled from patriotic feeling and could not utter the word 'England' without a sneer, were combining to betray their country to the Nazis. The instinct of the British people in the face of threat was to resist it, since that was what both duty and love required. But the muddled selfishness of the upper class and the snobbish sarcasm of their intellectual betters worked against the common people; the first making capitulation more probable, the second making capitulation look like political virtue in any case. Orwell's essay was a passionate attempt to show that the ordinary people were right.

[1] George Orwell, *The Lion and the Unicorn: Socialism and the English Genius*, London, 1941.

They could be trusted precisely because they were motivated by neither the self-interest of the upper class nor the self-righteousness of the intellectuals, but by the only thing that mattered, namely an undemonstrative love of their country.

Orwell's essay was as far as could then be imagined from the nationalist rants of the Nazis or the Communists' kitsch invocations of the proletarian future. It was a defence of patriotism, not as hatred of the other, but as love of what is ours. In a way nationalism and patriotism lie at the opposite poles of our attachments. Nationalism (at least in the inflamed version then prominent) displays a fear and contempt towards other forms of life. It is vigilant to the point of paranoia, and quickly turns on the 'enemy within', and indeed often depends on the story of an enemy within for its credibility, as Nazism did. Patriotism is based on respect and love for the form of life that we have. It seeks to include, not to exclude, and to combine in the face of external threat. A patriot respects the patriotism of others, including that of the enemy.

Orwell hoped to persuade the left-wing intellectuals of his day to jettison their treasonable anti-patriotism and to join in the defence of their country. He did not succeed entirely, as we know from the Cambridge spies.[2]

---

[2] See especially Ben Macintyre, *A Spy Among Friends*, London, 2014, describing Kim Philby and his network.

But his essay speaks to us still, as the voice of sanity in a time of madness. It tells us that patriotism is the *sine qua non* of survival, and that it arises spontaneously in the ordinary human heart. It does not depend upon any grand narrative of triumph of the kind put about by the fascists and the communists, but grows from the habits of free association that we British have been fortunate to inherit. It is this kind of patriotism that we stand in need of at this moment in our history, and in this chapter I will briefly say what it amounts to.

My subject is the identity that unites, or should unite, the British people now. However, even if the British are increasingly ignorant of their country's past, their loyalties have a kind of historical depth that resists every attempt to rub them to the wafer-thin time-slice of the now. We live with two rival conceptions of our past, standing to either side of the central icon, like warring heraldic beasts. On one side there is the proud people, who defended their 'sceptred isle' for a millennium, during the last centuries of which, in a burst of self-confidence, they carried trade, self-government and law around the world. On the other side there is the race of grasping imperialists, who spread chaos abroad and conflict at home, in pursuit of world domination.

The two caricatures are those given by the blimps and the intellectuals, as Orwell saw them, and of course both build upon truths as well as falsehoods. In recent academic writing it is the 'grasping imperialist' who has prevailed, and the history taught in our schools is broadly leftist history, which dwells on the abusive Stuart monarchy, the conflicts between the English and the Scots, the Highland clearances, the oppression of the Irish and the Indians, and the miseries of the industrial working class. Its heroes range from the more or less unknown Wat Tyler of the Peasants' Revolt via the Tolpuddle Martyrs and the Chartists of Victorian England to Mohandas Gandhi of the Indian independence movement, and it tells the story of 'liberties wrung and extorted bit by bit from arbitrary power'.[3] If this version of history has anything positive to say about the times in which we live, it is that they are times of 'liberation' and 'resistance', in which the noble tradition of revolt is being taken forward to its rightful conclusion in a society without distinctions of class, race or gender.

The history taught in my grammar school sixty years ago was the 'proud islanders' version. After all, we had recently won a difficult war against a dangerous enemy and in doing so had made the world safer for everyone, the Germans included. The curriculum dwelt upon successes, such as the defeat of the Spanish Armada, the saving of our Protestant inheritance during the Glorious Revolution of 1688, and the final undoing of Napoleon. But it offered instructive

[3] The words of the Liberal Member of Parliament Robert Lowe, in 1878.

moments of failure too, like the death of Captain Scott in the Antarctic or that of General Gordon at Khartoum, from which we learned that to face death with dignity was more noble than to triumph over enemies, however justified the triumph might be. The true patriot is not only a merciful victor, but a dignified loser too.

Of course there are other versions, besides those two caricatures, and it is a noteworthy fact about our country that those with designs on its present have generally been inspired to adopt a vision of its past. This habit was already established at the Restoration in 1660, with a spate of Royalist histories devoted to Charles the Martyr, and an equal accumulation of Commonwealth narratives dwelling on Stuart tyranny and the Parliamentary defence of our 'ancient liberties' and the Common Law. In a celebrated book the historian Sir Herbert Butterfield traced the emergence of a 'Whig interpretation of history', as one of the shaping forces of our national narrative from the Glorious Revolution to the present day.[4] According to this interpretation our recent history has been a story of progress, moving always from ignorance to knowledge, from servitude to emancipation, from conflict to reconciliation and from want to material sufficiency. To belong fully to the British idea, according to the Whig version, is to join the march of progress, and to root

[4] Herbert Butterfield, *The Whig Interpretation of History*, London, 1931.

13

out the benighted customs and superstitions that cloud the vision of the future. An updated version of the Whig narrative shaped Danny Boyle's opening ceremony for the 2012 London Olympics, and was gratefully received by many of the public as an expression of the cheerful good nature and unostentatious optimism of the British people. The fact that it was pure fantasy was of no real interest to the joyful crowds who witnessed it.

The Whig interpretation has been countered by a Tory version, according to which our history has been a process of deduction, a slow, steady extraction of institutions and liberties from the ancient gifts of monarchy, Christianity and the Common Law. Where the Whig version dwells on a record of progress and emancipation, the Tory version dwells on settlement and institutions. Both look backwards, in order to offer a story of how we have become what we are. There is truth in both stories, and sense in them only when they are seen in their full political contexts, as ways of recruiting loyalty to the place where we are.

The same is true for subsequent versions of the national story. During the early years of the twentieth century the rewriting of history with the socialist message buried deep within it became a kind of orthodoxy on the left,[5] while the shift to the right in the post-Thatcher

---

[5] Particularly influential were the popular histories of H. G. Wells and Sidney and Beatrice Webb, as well as R. H. Tawney's *Religion and the Rise of Capitalism*, London, 1926.

period has been as much the work of historians such as David Starkey, Niall Ferguson and Andrew Roberts as of political philosophers and think tanks. There is something about our culture that tempts political activists in this backward-looking direction. Even champions of the labour movement like E. P. Thompson and Raymond Williams look back on the past – in their case, of the working class – assured in their hearts that the present condition of their country can be understood only as the outcome of a long process of 'struggle', which they describe with regretful tenderness.[6] Likewise conservative defenders of Parliamentary sovereignty and the Common Law dwell on the continuous development of those institutions over eight hundred years, and on the slow but sure increments by which their legitimacy has become unchallengeable.[7]

The mass movements of continental twentieth-century politics – Fascism, Communism, National Socialism – laid claim to the future as their legitimating purpose and the only thing that mattered. British patriotism, in response, looked backwards, telling itself stories that represent things as they are now through the lens of a long and vindicating history. And this habit Orwell

---

[6] E. P. Thompson, *The Making of the English Working Class*, London, 1963; Raymond Williams, *Culture and Society, 1780–1950*, London, 1958.

[7] The classic here is F. W. Maitland, *The Constitutional History of England*, London, 1908.

perceived and advocated, as part of what he saw as our national gentleness.

In a previous book – *England: An Elegy* – I made clear that I lean towards the more forgiving view of our national history, or at least of the English part of it.[8] That was a book about England, designed more as a farewell to the country I knew than as a welcome to the new order that has begun to replace it. Nevertheless, much that I wrote has a bearing on Britain, as it returns to a condition of self-government in a world of rapid and unforeseen change. In particular I identified, in the history of England, a way of institution-building that was inseparable at every point from the attachment to the land and the desire to endow the land with the character of home. It mattered that the land was surrounded and protected by water, that it had a temperate and changeable climate, that it had been settled by a mixture of people whose languages had been synthesized to produce a dialect with a vocabulary twice the size of its immediate neighbours. And it mattered that the law of England was conceived as the law of the *land*, and not of any king, court or government that had taken temporary charge of it.

In the course of their history the English accepted monarchs of Norman, French, Scottish, Welsh, Dutch

---

[8] *England: An Elegy*, London, 2001. The vision that I adumbrate there is given some substance by Robert Tombs, in his magisterial *The English and Their History*, London, 2014.

and German origin, even monarchs such as George I who spoke no English, or monarchs like Cromwell who were not monarchs at all. They accepted them largely because they viewed their monarchs as creatures, and not creators, of the law. With the exception of Cromwell, each sovereign represented himself as entitled by law to his dominion, and – more importantly – as *subject* to the law and bound to uphold it. (It is true that the Stuarts hesitated over this matter, but they paid the price of their hesitation.) The point was made by the thirteenth-century judge Henry de Bracton, in his influential book on 'The Laws and Customs of England', written in Latin around 1220 and revised some thirty years later. The king, Bracton argued, lies below the law since it is the law that appoints him. Bracton was not philosophizing: he was articulating the rooted English understanding of law, as something objective, permanent, and part of the furniture of the country, something not invented but discovered. His argument was repeated and elaborated by the great jurist and Chief Justice, Sir Edward Coke, whose *Commentary upon Littleton*, published in 1628, staunchly defended the Common Law as binding on all within the kingdom, the king himself included. In due course, as the country expanded to include the Scots and the Irish, that conception of law was spread to them also – even though the Scots retained, and retain to this day, their own territorial jurisdiction.

Likewise religiously inspired conflicts in our country have from the earliest days involved an attempt to assert sovereignty over the Church in the interests of the secular power, and to insist that the Church *in* England is also the Church *of* England. All three words in that title are of equal importance. The enthusiasm released by Luther and Calvin led to violence in Britain, as elsewhere in Europe, comparatively mild though the violence was. However, when the Church of England had renounced all allegiance to Rome and accepted the monarch as its head, and when the boiling tides of godly passion had receded from our beautiful churches, leaving them stripped of their ornaments and dressed in puritan garments of plaster and stone – when the unacceptable 'in' had been replaced by the agreeable 'of', the English Church declared itself Protestant, while adopting a 'Book of Common Prayer' which in its Holy Communion is all but indistinguishable from the Roman Catholic Mass. Many of its members described their Church as 'Catholic and Reformed'. They continue to profess their belief in 'the Holy Catholic Church' and 'the Communion of Saints', and the Eucharist is more or less identical with the Roman Catholic version, distinguished largely by a metaphysical commentary that ridicules the old nonsense in new nonsense of its own. Although the Church in Scotland became, at the Reformation, explicitly Calvinist, it too shaped itself as a national Church, described since the sixteenth century as the Church of Scotland, or simply the Kirk.

The country emerged from the wars of religion to become a 'Union' of England and Scotland, which had already been ruled for a century under a single Crown. Thanks to the Act of Settlement of 1701, the law of this country stipulates that the Crown must be conferred on or inherited by a Protestant. How significant is this fact? Some historians, led in recent times by Linda Colley, have seen Protestantism as a homogenizing force, establishing a common culture across the kingdom, and thereby per-mitting a distinctively 'British' identity to emerge in place of the narrowly conceived English and Scottish identi-ties which had been inflamed when the two countries were at war.[9] But perhaps it was just as much the other way round – that the British understood Protestantism in terms of their expanding idea of nationality, rather than seeing their nationality in terms of the Protestant faith. They *called* themselves Protestants, certainly, but not so loudly as to deny the English Church's claim to be both Catholic and heir to the Apostolic Succession. And they abhorred the Pope – though, as Daniel Defoe remarked, the streets of London were, at the time of the 'no Popery' riots, full of 'stout fellows willing to fight to the death against Popery without knowing whether it

[9] Linda Colley, *Britons: Forging the Nation, 1707–1837*, New Haven, 1992.

be a man or a horse'. The contest with Rome remained
what it had always been – a dispute over jurisdiction and
sovereignty, and a tenacious adherence to local custom
and historic compromise as the true sources of legitimate government. It is only an exaggeration to say that
the attitude of the British people to the Bishop of Rome
at the end of the seventeenth century anticipates that to
the Treaty of Rome today. Both attitudes affirm the sovereignty of the people against the impertinent claims of
an external power.

The idea of the Protestant Succession should therefore
be construed in that spirit. For a century or more before
the Act of Settlement was passed, Roman Catholicism
had meant allegiance to Rome, to Spain or to France,
in conflicts that were critical for the future of the country. The British people have cared less about the origins,
titles or sanity of their kings and queens than about their
commitment to upholding the law of the land – the very
law by which the monarchs hold office, and which can be
used if necessary to eject them. The true meaning of the
law of succession, as British people would now interpret
it, is not that the monarch should be a Protestant in any
real sense of the term – after all, of how many people
alive today could that be truly said? It is that he or she
should be wholly and exclusively committed to upholding the law and sovereignty of the kingdom. We see
clearly in the vestiges of the conflict between Catholic

and Protestant in Northern Ireland today, that it has been about sovereignty, not religion, and concerns rival answers to the question 'Who is my neighbour?' And in the crises of the twentieth century the active involvement of a patriotic royal family has been one of the most powerful reminders that we belong together in this place that is ours. In the eyes of the people the assertion of national identity and togetherness remains the principal duty of the Crown; and their willing undertaking of this duty is the reason why the Queen and the royal family remain so firmly anchored in the people's affections.

The Glorious Revolution of 1688, the adoption of William and Mary as monarchs, and the Act of Union with Scotland of 1707, were followed by years of comparative peace, in which it was widely accepted that, 'no Popery' apart, religion had become a ceremonial affair, a necessary way of dignifying important public events, and a private devotion that offered consolation to those who needed it, but which was not the real source of social or political unity. Writing in the *Spectator* in 1712, Joseph Addison put the point succinctly: 'we have in England a particular bashfulness in everything that regards religion'. The topic had become as unmentionable as sex or hygiene, and has remained so until this day. Maybe that was not so true in Scotland, with its vehement Calvinist and Presbyterian legacy. Nevertheless the philosopher David Hume made a similar point, writing in 1748 that his countrymen (in which term he included both the English and the Scots) displayed the 'most cool indifference in religious matters, that is to be found in any nation of the world'.[10] By the mid-nineteenth century, religious fervour was disappearing both north and south of the border. The census of 1851 showed that already only 50 per cent of British people were regular worshippers, a figure that dropped to 25 per cent in some city areas. And a century later George Orwell was able to write that the British people are essentially without religious belief, even though retaining a core of Christian feeling.[11] This Christian feeling shows itself in a general charitableness towards those in distress, and an easygoing spirit of cooperation in the face of emergencies. And Orwell wished to build around this somewhat negative account of our national virtues a description of 'who we are' that would be acceptable to all those on whom his country depended in the war against Hitler.

Likewise I am seeking a description of 'who we are' that will serve to unite the citizens of our country behind its renewed status, as an independent sovereign state. And like Orwell I am drawn to the spiritual residue that remains, when all the contentious claims of religion and ideology have been laid aside, and only the day-to-day

---

[10] David Hume, 'Of National Characters', 1748.
[11] Orwell, The Lion and the Unicorn, op. cit.

habits of neighbourliness remain. Orwell believed that this would be enough, and I agree with him.

Of course, the ethnically unified, class-conscious society of which Orwell wrote has largely disappeared. Mass immigration and multiculturalism have profoundly unsettled us, and the close-knit working-class communities of Orwell's time have been dispersed or marginalized. Nevertheless it is my belief that we can, in our new and sovereign condition, address the problem of social integration. For the quotidian neighbourliness that is so familiar to us is not a shallow thing. It is the product of a long experiment in community, issuing in a culture of 'side-by-sidedness' that has its equivalents elsewhere, but which is also the way in which British people resolve their conflicts and cooperate in building trust. For us, political choices are underpinned by the sovereignty of the people, mediated by Parliament and the Common Law, and the people are united because they share a home and a long-established way of governing it. We are not unique in this: on the contrary, we are one instance of a European ideal, the ideal of neighbourhood as the source of political order. Although we have been subject to an experiment in religious and ethnic diversity, it remains true that national sovereignty and the sense of place are the cornerstones of our social capital and the foundation of the home that we have built with it. Who we are is *where* we are.

Home is a personalizing force: it endows objects, customs and institutions with a moral character, so that we respond to them as we respond to one another, 'I to thou'. This, I believe, lies at the heart of our experience of identity. The British people, like their Dutch and Scandinavian cousins, are 'joiners' by nature: they relate more easily to clubs, regiments, schools, pubs and teams than to individual human beings. Or rather, they find human relations more natural, easier to conduct without embarrassment, when they occur between people already joined by threads of membership.[12] However far back we look into our history, we find those 'little platoons' of which Burke wrote: focal points of local but durable loyalties.[13] From the guilds to the trade unions, from the cathedral chapters to the colliery brass bands, from the public schools to the Boy Scouts and the Women's Institute, from the Worshipful Company of Farriers to the Institute of Directors, from the Highland Games to the Scottish Society of Antiquaries, you will find the same 'clubbable' instinct, which prefers custom, formality and ritualized membership to the hullabaloo of crowds, and which imposes a quiet and genial discipline in place of spontaneous social emotion.

[12] The Americans share this character, which was singled out by Tocqueville as responsible for the extraordinary stability of the American settlement, democracy and equality notwithstanding: *Democracy in America*, 1835.

[13] Edmund Burke, *Reflections on the Revolution in France*, 1791.

Of course, the crowd emotions are also there, and in football, which has been the centre of our holiday relaxations since Elizabethan times, the competitive contest has become a central drama in the rivalry of tribes. Even here, however, an ethos of restrained membership generally prevails over the desire for riot, and the fan rejoices more in his unassuming loyalty to the team than in triumphs in the stadium.[14] Even at a match between Celtic and Rangers, when the fans scream hatred and loathing across the pitch, it is for the moment and for form's sake only, and less important than the replay later in the pub.

For the Welsh and the Scots as much as the English their country has been a home, settled by small communities, teams and clubs, in which churches and chapels thrive among many more secular forms of recreation. Their identity has been formed through a personal relationship with a place – a place consecrated by the things that happen there, and which happen in the same unfussy way as a game of football. The feeling of the Welsh for their settled way of life has been captured for all time by Dylan Thomas, in his great 'play for voices' *Under Milk Wood* (1954), while such classics as *The Diary of a Nobody* (1892) by George and Weedon Grossmith and *The Wind in the Willows* (1908) by Kenneth Grahame have provided English readers with a soothing vision of a place that will

---

[14] See Nick Hornby, *Fever Pitch*, London, 1996.

always be there in their dreams and aspirations, however far from it they are in reality.

It is difficult to transcribe this kind of identity, derived from place and neighbourhood rather than from faith or doctrine, into a credo. Against the fascists and the communists, who offered a march into the future behind a waving banner of doctrine, Orwell could appeal only to impressions, memories and scattered residues of life. In an essay entitled 'England Your England' he was reduced to defining his country as a bundle of sensations:

> The clatter of clogs in the Lancashire mill towns, the to-and-fro of the lorries on the Great North Road, the queues outside the Labour Exchanges, the rattle of pin tables in the Soho pubs, the old maids biking to Holy Communion through the mists of the autumn morning – all these are not only fragments, but *characteristic* fragments, of the English scene.[15]

But all those sensations, apart from the lorries on what is now a motorway, belong in the past, and owe their importance only to the fact that an accomplished writer happened to notice them. The point is that Orwell was describing not a people but a place, and at the same time identifying that place in terms of the personal relations

[15] 'England Your England', in *The Lion and the Unicorn*, op. cit.

that flourished there. For Orwell his country was not a nation or a creed or a language but a home.

Things at home don't need an explanation. They are there because they are there. It was one of the most remarkable features of the English, and until recently of the Scots too, that they required so little explanation of their customs and institutions. They bumbled on, without anyone asking the reason why or anyone being able, if asked, to provide it. Continental observers often accuse us of disrespect for reason, and an unwillingness to think things through, as now in the Brexit vote. But if the result of thinking things through is paradox, why should reason require it?

The French thought things through at their Revolution, and the result was accurately summarized by Robespierre: 'the despotism of liberty'. Impenetrable contradiction is what you must expect, when you try to start from scratch, and refuse to recognize that custom, tradition, law and a spirit of undemanding cooperation are the best that human beings can obtain by way of government. So for several centuries we have been content with an unwritten constitution, a Parliament whose powers remain undefined, a form of sovereignty that can be traced to no specific institution and no single person, a system of justice in which the most important laws are not written down, and patterns of local administration that cannot be explained even by those who operate them. And when politicians attempt to rectify the matter, so as to impose rational order in the place of reasonable disarray, they usually end with a greater mess than they started from, as with Tony Blair's 'reforms' to the judicial system or his creation of a Scottish Parliament without thinking to create an English Parliament that would balance it.

Home is a place where you can be yourself and do your own thing. Respect the rituals and the household gods, and for the rest you can please yourself. Therefore when people feel at home they allow themselves hobbies and eccentricities. They become amateurs, experts and cranks. They collect stamps, butterflies or biscuit tins; they compete in growing vegetables, breeding dogs and racing pigeons, and join with their neighbours in order to make music, play skittles or build steam engines. The eccentricity of the British people has followed as a matter of course, from the fact that they have been at home in their world and safe there.

The same is true of their amateurism. It was not only the empire that was acquired by private ventures, and in 'a fit of absence of mind'.[16] Almost the entire social order of the country arose in recent times from private initiatives. Schools, colleges and universities; municipalities, hospitals, theatres; festivals and even the army regiments

[16] Sir John Seeley, *The Expansion of England*, London, 1938.

tell the same story: some public-spirited amateur, rais-
ing funds, setting out principles, acquiring premises, and
then bequeathing the achievement to trustees or to the
Crown, with the state appearing, if at all, only after the
event, in order to guarantee the survival and propagation
of good works that it would never have initiated by itself.
That is the way of people who are at home, and who
refuse to be bossed about by those whom they regard
as outsiders. Their attitude to officialdom reflects their
conviction that, if something needs to be done, then the
person to do it is you. Even the sovereign, embarking on
some charitable enterprise, has done so, as a rule, as a
private individual, creating another autonomous institution outside the control of the state. (Witness the Royal
Society, the Queen Elizabeth's Foundation for Disabled
People, the Duke of Edinburgh awards, the Prince's
Trust, the Princess Royal Trust for carers, and so on;
the Queen is now patron to over 500 charities, and the
Royals support 3,000 charities around the world.)

Networks of self-help are natural, and exist wherever
the state has not extinguished them – as it extinguished
them in Revolutionary France and later in Nazi and
Communist Europe. France recovered from the totalitarian aspirations of the Revolutionaries, but largely
because Napoleon recreated the fabric of civil society
through a network of state commissions. In this connection we should take note of the contrast drawn by Robert

Tombs between two 'myths' of national identity – the Magna Carta myth, which became a fundamental part of the British self-image during the nineteenth century, and the 'Vanguard' myth that has played such an important role in overcoming civil conflict in France, Italy and Germany.[17] The Magna Carta myth tells us that those with power, even if they wear the crown, must always answer to the people beneath them, and – should they overstep the mark – must face the tribunal of their subjects, as King John did in 1215 at Runnymede. The Vanguard myth speaks of the legitimate use of power by those – the experts, the intellectuals, the liberators – who have the knowledge required to lead the people to a salvation that they could never achieve on their own.

The Vanguard has supposedly risen above popular criticism, and is unchallengeable from any position other than its own. British sovereigns, by contrast, are always answerable, in the end, to the people beneath them. The contrast here is pertinent to the rival visions of Europe – that of the European Commission, which refuses to accept any divergence from its ultimate plan, and that of the British people, who see the European Union as an alliance of sovereign states, each of which ought to be accountable to the people from whom its sovereignty

---

[17] Robert Tombs, 'Europeanism and its Historical Myths', in David Abulafia, ed., *European Demos: A Historical Myth*, London, 2015.

derives. Hence the British people react with astonishment when electorates who vote in a referendum against the Union plan – as did the Dutch, the French and the Irish – are ignored or asked to vote again, or when elected governments in trouble, like those of Italy and Greece, are deprived of the options required for their national survival.

I will return to Tombs's distinction. But it must be borne in mind at this juncture since it defines two distinct narratives of legitimacy, each of which has had a part to play in the evolving situation of our continent. Myths are not simply falsehoods: they are parables that contain a concealed truth, a truth about people's aspirations and the way in which they realize them. Napoleon, leaning on the Vanguard myth, brought education and religion under the aegis of the state, knitted the torn fabric of civil society, and created a top-down system of offices and institutions on which successive French Republics have depended to this day. He reorganized the law on Roman-law principles, emphasizing the edicts of the sovereign power over the judgements of the courts. And he spread the resulting *Code Napoléon* by conquest across much of Europe.

In our country, by contrast, private foundations, amateur circles, clubs and friendly societies were reshaping civil society without explicit help from government, while law remained in essence common law, extracted from the judgements of the courts and not dictated by the legislature. It was not the state but the churches, chapels and philanthropic associations of citizens that brought education to the people. It was not the state but friendly societies, building societies and charitable employers such as Robert Owen and the Cadbury family, which first provided the industrial workforce with housing. It was not the state but People's Dispensaries and volunteer hospitals that first brought the benefits of modern medicine to the poor. The real advances in health care in the nineteenth century were due on the one hand to the determination of Florence Nightingale to make nursing into a science and a profession, and on the other hand to the doctors and surgeons who founded the Provincial Medical and Surgical Association in 1832 – a body that was to become the British Medical Association in 1856, by which time it had already established its path-breaking journal and prompted Parliament to take an interest in the nation's health.

Societies of amateurs have flourished elsewhere in Europe, notably in the Scandinavian and Dutch-speaking parts and under the aegis of the Austro-Hungarian Empire.[18] Nevertheless our own case has been exceptional. For – as I shall argue in more detail in Chapter Five – our legal system gives credibility to private

[18] For a useful summary see Stefan-Ludwig Hoffmann, *Civil Society*, London, 2006.

initiatives and protects them from the jealousy of leg-
islators. As a result there has grown up in our kingdom,
and in England especially, a unique attitude to officialdom, and to the rules and regulations that modern
governments impose. While the British people have
always been charmed by ceremony and tradition, they
also know them to be human inventions. Authority is
intangible; it can be identified with no real human being
and certainly not with an official in uniform. Hence the
love of ancient customs, precedents and rituals has always
been tempered by an urge to laugh at them – not mali-
ciously, but gently and ironically, by way of recognizing
their merely human provenance. The empire reached its
zenith of pomp at the same time as Gilbert and Sullivan
wrote the operas that satirized its ruling offices: the
peerage, the judiciary, the army, the navy and even roy-
alty itself. And the new hierarchies of government in our
democratic age are accepted through a similar debunk-
ing in *Yes, Minister* and *The Thick Of It*.

This attitude to officialdom derives in part from the
peculiar status of the ordinary person in common-law
jurisdictions. The celebrated writ of *Habeas Corpus*, issued
in the king's name, commands whoever has impris-
oned a subject of the Crown to deliver that person to
the king's court for trial. This writ is issued on petition
from whoever can show cause, and enshrines an ancient
common-law right to liberty of the person, enjoyed by

33

all his majesty's subjects. The king's role is to guarantee this liberty, and the writ reminds him of this. Much has been written about *Habeas Corpus*, and its effect over the centuries in enshrining individual liberty at the heart of English-speaking justice.[19] It is one aspect of a general tendency in English law since its first clear emergence in the early Middle Ages, which is to develop as a defence in the hands of the individual subject, rather than a weapon with which to command and oppress him. I return to this topic in Chapter Five, but it should be borne in mind since it offers a partial explanation of a crucial factor in recent events, which is the refusal of the British people to be bossed about by those on whom, in their view at least, they have conferred no right of government.

Although our freedom is rooted in the Common Law and in the long and sometimes confrontational dialogue between the Crown and Parliament, it owes its prominence as a national icon to the evolution of the country since the Napoleonic wars. By the time of the first Reform Bill of 1832, which extended the franchise to large sections of middle-class men, the

---

[19] See for example Anthony Gregory, *The Power of Habeas Corpus in America*, Cambridge, Cambridge University Press, 2013; George Parkin Grant, *English-Speaking Justice*, New Brunswick, 1974. A version of *Habeas Corpus* was introduced into Scotland by the then Parliament of Scotland in the Criminal Procedure Act, 1701. For the complexities of Scots Law during the eighteenth-century transition from the old Roman-law system to the current hybrid, see Sir Walter Scott's eloquent and moving account in *The Heart of Midlothian*, and in particular chapter XXIII.

identity of 'the United Kingdom' was a settled fact. The Scots and the Protestant Irish accepted to be included in the revised conception of the country, and the Act of Union with Ireland of 1800, followed by the Catholic Emancipation Act of 1829, invited the Irish fully to share in the deal. The years that followed were not harmonious: the Highland clearances continued, as did the oppression of the Irish smallholders, exacerbating the disastrous famine of 1845–52. So too did the mass migration to the industrial towns, the exploitation of child labour, and the dehumanizing factory regimes.

However, as I noted above, the British do not, as a rule, confront problems with an attitude of resignation and laissez-faire. Their instinct is to combine in order to solve them. The Factory Acts, the Friendly Societies, Building Societies, church schools and people's dispensaries, the Chartist movement, the second Reform Bill extending the franchise to large sections of working-class men, the growth of the Labour movement – these and many other social and political initiatives overcame the worst of the problems in England, and ensured that the pre-political 'we' of Britain was strong enough to reconcile the many resentments. The oppressive system of land-ownership in Ireland, and the contempt of the largely Protestant English land-owning class for their Catholic and Irish tenants, meant that this 'we' would be regarded by the Catholic Irish thereafter with justified anger. Only now, after two centuries of bitterness, are our two countries approaching some kind of accommodation, and it is one of the most powerful arguments for the European Union that it has facilitated this process.

Despite that great wound, the nineteenth century led to a United Kingdom that, by the mid-twentieth century, was proud of its independence, and sustained by the loyalty of its four constituent nations. Britons came to see themselves as living in a 'free country', and to regard their freedom as a quality of the institutions under which they live, and the space in which those institutions operate. They were, for the most part, aware of their good fortune in enjoying a universal education system and a free health service, and they acknowledged, despite a dissenting minority, that their Parliamentary institutions and constitutional monarchy were the guarantee of order and stability. But all those great benefits were secondary in their minds to the quite special freedom that they enjoyed in their daily lives.

Those lucky enough to be able to travel encountered this freedom, like a refreshing breeze, when they arrived 'home' from 'abroad', and sensed that they were now in safe hands. Freedom was seen as an inheritance, a feature of a way of life, not to be understood in terms of the multiplicity of options, still less in a list of civil rights. It was a shared way of being, founded in mutual trust, and the product of institutions that were not created in a day but had been passed on from generation to generation as public possessions. The free citizen was marked by a proud independence, a respect for others, and a sense of responsibility for the common way of life and the choices it protected. Fair-mindedness, acceptance of eccentricity and a reluctance to take offence, combined with an aversion towards abuse and slander – all these were attributes of the British, and belonged to them by virtue of public institutions in which they placed their trust and which they were tutored to defend both in thought and deed against those who might otherwise destroy them. Such citizens fought for the freedom of their country, and for their own freedom as part of it. And that, in a nutshell, was the British character.

Nothing in history stays still, however. Years of peace and prosperity, the decline of the Christian faith, mass migration and the spread of global trade and communications – these and other vast changes have produced a generation of young people more attuned to networks that connect them to their peers than to the liberties that their grandparents fought for. They have not been confronted in their lives with the emergency to which patriotism is the only cogent response, although the jihadists are trying hard to rectify this. So what broad conception of the British settlement and British character can we now rely upon, in exhorting our compatriots to identify with their country, as an independent body politic in a place of its own?

It is precisely in confronting this question that recent politicians have made their greatest mistakes. Gordon Brown, as Prime Minister, spoke much about British values, and tried in various speeches to define them. Ofsted, in charge of the school curriculum, has picked up the challenge and tells us that British values include democracy, the rule of law, individual freedom and tolerance towards all faiths and none. And of course that fits with the account that I have given, and the account that Orwell gave seventy-five years ago. And it shows a welcome, if belated, recognition of the duty of immigrants to tolerate those among whom they settle, whatever the differences of custom and faith. But it defines Britishness in terms of values, rather than the other way round.

It is precisely what distinguishes us – this island home and the political institutions that have domesticated it – that has created the particular kind of freedom and togetherness that make the Magna Carta myth believable. Democratic accountability, individual freedom, law abidingness and toleration were acquired over many centuries and not without bitter conflict. But we embrace them because they speak to us of *how things are done here*, in the place that is ours. We want newcomers to belong to this place. And while that may involve radical changes in their ways of doing things, and an adoption of the stated values, it is not enough to acquire those values, if in doing so they do not acquire the attachment to Britain as their home. This attachment is the crucial thing, and lies deeper than all the customs and ambitions that arise from it.

The case is comparable to that of a family, sharing a single home. Many of the habits and attitudes of a family are shared, but the members of the family are not at home merely because those habits and attitudes surround them. Other homes may have similar habits: it is not the habits that make the home, but the home that makes the habits. People behave in this shared and predictable way because they belong to the same place. Belonging is the *basic* fact, and may admit of no further explanation. And this is as true for young people as it is for their parents and grandparents.

Hence, while we can say much about our unique legal and political inheritance, it is the image of the country itself, as a settled spot of earth, that crystallizes the prevailing sense of who we are. It is a commonplace that our temperate climate and uncertain weather are connected to our phlegmatic character, and are partly responsible for our habit of downplaying emergencies. But the influence of the country's physical attributes goes far deeper than that. The extraordinary variety of soils, the rock formations, the abundance of estuaries and inlets, the surrounding ocean currents, the accessibility of each part of the mainland to every other – such factors have created a unique experience of place, which expresses itself in our institutions and laws, in our attitude to the rest of the world and in the daily life of our people.[20]

The influence goes both ways: the country shaped its inhabitants, who in turn shaped the country, not least through the bottom-up approach to law and property rights that has been the most conspicuous legacy of the Anglo-Saxon forms of government. The English and Welsh countryside is criss-crossed by boundaries and rights of way. Hedges and dry-stone walls make the patchwork quilt that is so admired by those who don't have the problem of farming it. Although many of the enclosures were the result of Acts of Parliament, they reinforced the rule of private ownership. It is only in the twentieth century, with the creation of the Forestry Commission in 1919 and the expropriations required by the two world wars, that the state became the largest landowner. And all that people love in our landscape depends still upon boundaries – boundaries that both affirm the rights of the landowner and remain frequently permeable to the rest of us.

[20] See Harry Mount, *How England Made the English: From Hedgerows to Heathrow*, New York, 2012.

Of course, the same cannot be said of Scotland, where the beauty of the Highlands depends precisely on their unbounded quality, rising above the valleys where vestigial walls and sheep-pens, rubbed out by time, mark boundaries that have disappeared and populations that have vanished. But the Scots remain as attached to their landscape as the English to theirs, and it has an equal place in their art and literature, from the poems of 'Ossian' and the novels of Walter Scott to the music of Sir Peter Maxwell Davies and Sir James MacMillan.

The bottom-up approach to law and property goes hand in hand with local opposition to overarching plans. It is to this that we owe the higgledy-piggledy contours of the English village and the market town, and it is the effort to preserve those contours that has led both to the resistance to modernist architecture and to the attempt to preserve patina at all costs — even the attempt to *build* patina, as at Poundbury in Dorset or Knockroon in Scotland, an attempt that belongs to the great project, embodied in the person of Sir John Betjeman, of treating the entire country as a toy-town village.[21]

Hence it is not only our towns and villages that owe their appeal to their unplanned neighbourliness. The same is true of the southern countryside, which

---

[21] No detailed account of what the physical contours of our country have meant to recent generations of British people can ignore the work of Sir John Betjeman, in describing, celebrating and satirizing its deep deposits of meaning.

emerged from an evolving consensus in which neigh-
bourly friction and common-law litigation were far more
important than top-down plans. Likewise, the passion
for the picturesque led to some radical attempts to plan
the countryside, often with scant regard for its existing
occupants. But the intention was to create another version of the spontaneous order that was being destroyed.
The same is true of our post-war planning laws, which
have had the preservation of the countryside as their
most important purpose.

Although most of us live in cities, we retain the idea
of the countryside as the place where we really belong,
the place to which we will one day return, to take up
the tranquil rhythms from which we were sundered
by the modern turmoil. That is why *The Wind in the
Willows* – that invocation of a landscape in which only
harmless animals reside – remains so popular, and why
the British imagination finds itself naturally at home in
Hogwarts, as imagined by J. K. Rowling; that is why
The Archers, even after its takeover by urban mischief-
makers, retains its (largely urban) audience. Nor is it
only popular culture that endows our countryside with
an iconic significance. At least since the Enlightenment
our serious literature, art and music have been consist-
ently pastoral in their inspiration. Without the countryside and all that it means there would be no Coleridge
or Wordsworth, no Jane Austen, no Brontë sisters, no

42

Walter Scott, no George Eliot or Thomas Hardy, no Elgar, Vaughan Williams or Ivor Gurney, no Constable, Crome or Turner. When, in the nineteenth century, people began to confront the questions posed by the mass migration to the cities and the rise of the factories, therefore, it was in part with a view to protecting the countryside from further spoliation at the hands of the industrialists.

This feeling for the countryside has profoundly influenced urbanization in both England and Scotland. From the eighteenth century onwards developers have provided potted versions of the rural environment – green squares, small parks, tree-lined streets, sometimes gardens front and rear – with scant respect for the kind of economy of land use that we witness in Italy or France. The nineteenth-century cities were built either as collections of suburbs or as model industrial settlements, such as Robert Owen's New Lanark in Scotland, and the Cadbury family's Bourneville near Birmingham. They grew from a subconscious sense that to build is to intrude on nature, and that the intrusion must always be apologized for. As the cities expanded so too did the apology, an attitude that led at last to the 'garden city' movement of Sir Ebenezer Howard.

That movement is alive today, one force in the great controversy over land use precipitated by our housing crisis. And it illustrates a singular fact about the British people, which is that they are unhappy if they are not living on the ground.[22] However poor they are, British people will avoid high-rise apartment blocks and strive to live where they can open a door onto their piece of territory. The building societies and friendly societies came about in order to satisfy this need to settle in a place of one's own, and ultimately to retire there, growing flowers in front of the house and vegetables behind. Our Garden Centres, gardening magazines, *Gardeners' Question Time* on the radio and a hundred other fragments, far more important than those noted in the passage quoted above from George Orwell, reveal the true heart of the British people, which is the place where they really are, where nobody has the right to disturb them, and where they can pick up a fork or a spade and thrust it into soil of their own.

Those feelings are as powerful today as they were when the industrial workforce first migrated to the cities. And they partly explain why the environmental movement arose so early in Britain. Already in 1844 Wordsworth was campaigning against the railways on behalf of his beloved Lake District. The barrister George Shaw-Lefevre founded the Commons, Open Spaces and Footpaths Preservation Society in 1865, and John Ruskin the Guild of St George

---

[22] See the research carried out by Nicholas Boys-Smith for Create Streets, research document 14 March 2014, www.createstreets.com.

in 1870. Societies were formed all across the country to protect the shrinking forests and the threatened coastlines. A disciple of Ruskin, Octavia Hill, combined with others to found the National Trust in 1895, and the fact that this private association now has 5 million members, for whom visits to the countryside are a vital source of relaxation and renewal, says something important about the real source of our national sentiment.

This iconizing of the landscape should not surprise us: the distinction between 'home' and 'abroad' is emphasized in every direction by the sea. The unique system of law and property rights that have guaranteed the peace of the United Kingdom are also inscribed on the land. Hedges and walls speak of private rights to exclude people; footpaths, bridleways and green lanes speak of the public refusal to be excluded. Ours is a negotiated countryside, one that belongs in a certain measure to all of us, and which has been shaped by a singular way of life and a native genius for compromise. Hence the founding, in 1935, of the Ramblers Association (now simply 'The Ramblers'), with over 100,000 members, dedicated to keeping the landscape open to those who wish to walk in it, and qualifying the property rights of landlords in favour of the recreational demands of the rest of us.

It was natural that, in the two world wars, the countryside should be identified as the symbol of 'what we are fighting for'. Paul and John Nash and Eric Ravilious gave us images of horse-drawn ploughs and quaintly coloured tractors amid copse-crowned fields, and these images were soon engraved in people's hearts and also taken up by the war ministry as beneficial propaganda. This was not a sudden visual awakening but simply the natural expression in times of stress of a feeling that had guided British sentiment since the dawn of the industrial revolution.

Sceptics will say that the image of the countryside is already in tatters, that the villages are now dormitories for the super-rich, and that the old way of life has died under the weight of agricultural subsidies, motorways, agri-business and the Labour Party's hostility to field sports. I believe that this is not so. Rural people do not live as they used to live; but they have adapted to their new circumstances and maintained the rhythms that the land itself dictates to them.[23] And when, in response to the Labour government's decision to ban traditional forms of hunting, the countryside decided to make its feelings known, the largest-ever march on the capital took place, with half a million law-abiding people converging on Westminster. This was the first nationwide uprising of country people against the urban elites since the Peasants' Revolt of 1381, and the first indication of the discontent that was to lead at last to the vote for Brexit.

[23] See my account of the small farming community where I live, *News from Somewhere*, London, 2004.

Such examples of popular protest raise an important question, however, and it is one that already troubled Orwell: can there really be patriotism on the left? Isn't the whole tendency of left-wing thought to repudiate those old forms of belonging, with their implicit hierarchies, their pieties, their deference in the face of established privilege and power? Isn't the goal to side with the working class, rather than the nation, which is in the hands of the bourgeois enemy? And if there is a further goal, is it not to create an international order, in which an egalitarian form of government erases the boundary between 'us' and 'them'? Should not our leftists be joining the social democrats of the European Union, and working for a new society in which the 'rural idiots' who marched in such numbers on London simply go on marching into the grave? That was certainly the attitude of the Labour Party at the time.

Orwell would not have agreed. He accepted the premise that socialists must organize in defence of the working class. But the workers themselves, he believed, are reluctant to identify their loyalties in class terms. The Marxist idea that the working 'class in itself' can become a revolutionary 'class for itself' is a piece of wishful thinking. The 'we' of the working class, Orwell believed, is the 'we' of the nation, of which the workers are the beating heart. They saw themselves, at the time when he wrote, as patriotic subjects, schooled to stand together

47

against oppression, and to recognize that solidarity does not mean the renunciation of loyalties and duties for the sake of some global nowhere, but the fight for justice here and now. In his more bitter moments Orwell saw the left-wing intellectuals as the enemy, whose commitment to utopia led them to despise the mere human beings who stood in its way.

Intellectuals on the left have by and large justified Orwell's suspicion. And in a small measure the disconnect between the left-wing intelligentsia and the working class was mirrored in the Brexit vote, when leading members of the Labour Party chose to ignore its traditional constituency, and to condemn the 'leave' vote as an expression of 'xenophobia'. It soon became clear, however, that the Labour Party will regain its status as a party of government only if it recognizes the residual patriotism of its traditional voters, and concedes that it is possible to be a working-class socialist, a believer in national sovereignty, and a normal decent human being, who is neither racist nor xenophobic when it comes to dealing with the wider world. The party therefore has the task that confronts us all, which is that of defining patriotism anew, so that every age group, every temperament and every career can belong to a shared first-person plural. In particular, it must revise its attitude to globalization, in order to acknowledge that the principal victim of the emerging global networks is the old working class.

There is another objection that might reasonably be made from the left, however, which is that I have given only one half of the picture, emphasizing the democratic instinct of the British and their propensity toward bottom-up forms of government. Like all people, however, the British recognize the need for order, planning and – in emergencies – a hierarchy of command. And in the post-war period, influenced both by the discipline of fighting and by the then current belief in the new socialist programmes, they were as given to the 'vanguard' way of thinking as the French and the Germans. Indeed, Orwell was an advocate of the planned economy, and when in 1973 Edward Heath took our country into the European Economic Community, as it then was, he relied on the experts and the forecasters to explain to the people that it was all part of a rational plan.

On the other hand we should not forget that the plan described by the experts was not the plan intended by the European politicians. The plan in the minds of its leading advocates was for new institutions of government, which would override national sovereignty in order to create a federal administration for the continent as a whole. Such a plan lies beyond anything that the British people would have accepted, had it been explained to them. Government planning, they believe, should be an exercise of sovereignty, not a step towards renouncing it. The plan is there in order to foster negotiated solutions and

long-term compromises. And our most cherished form
of planning, as embodied in the Town and Country
Planning Act of 1946, is not there to change the country into something else but rather to conserve the
country as we know it, and to ensure that we pass on to
future generations the precious landscapes and town-
scapes that are ours by right. The beautiful places in our
country were not, on the whole, produced by planning,
and that is why planning is needed to preserve them.

Even with the socialist plans of the post-war government there was no end point, no equivalent of the 'ever
closer union' promised by the European Treaty. There was
only a pooling of resources in the common interest, where
the common interest was defined by the people themselves, rather than by a clique of self-appointed leaders.

I shall return to this point in discussing the British conception of freedom. What is necessary now is to understand how our patriotic sentiment, defined in terms of
a home and the sovereign people who reside there, can
form the foundation of a creative response to Brexit.
Our sentiment of belonging must adapt to the many
changes that have occurred in our geopolitical status,
and to the disturbed balance of our kingdom, now that
Scottish demands for independence are a part of the political culture. And this sentiment must be distinguished
from those pathological forms of national pride that have
troubled our continent since the French Revolution.

3

NATIONS, NATIONALISM AND US

In modern conditions, in which governments rarely enjoy a majority vote, most of us in Western democracies are living under a government of which we don't approve. We accept to be ruled by laws and decisions made by politicians with whom we disagree, and whom we often deeply dislike. How is that possible? Why don't democracies regularly collapse, as people refuse to be governed by those they never voted for?

Clearly a modern democracy must be held together by something stronger than party politics. There has to be a 'first-person plural', a pre-political loyalty, which causes neighbours who voted in opposing ways to treat each other as fellow citizens, for whom the government is not 'mine' or 'yours' but 'ours', whether or not we approve of it. This first-person plural varies in strength, from fierce attachment in wartime, to casual acceptance on a Monday morning at work. But at some level it must be assumed if we are to accept a shared form of government.

A country's stability is enhanced by economic growth. But it depends far more upon this sense that we belong together, and that we will stand by each other during the real emergencies. In short, it relies on a legacy of social trust. Trust of this kind depends on a common territory, resolution in the face of external threat, and customs and institutions that foster collective decisions in response to the problems of the day. It is the *sine qua non* of enduring peace, and also the greatest asset of any people that possesses it, as we British have possessed it throughout the enormous changes that gave rise to the modern world.

There is a great difference between societies in which trust depends on personal acquaintance and family ties, and one, such as ours, in which trust exists between people who are strangers to each other. And people acquire trust in different ways. Urban elites build trust through career moves, joint projects and cooperation across borders. Like the aristocrats of old they often form networks without reference to national boundaries. They do not, on the whole, depend upon a particular place, a particular faith or a particular routine for their sense of membership, and in the immediate circumstances of modern life they can adapt to globalization without too much difficulty. In the Brexit vote they may have experienced little reluctance in saying yes to the European Union, since it threatens their way of life, if at all, only at the margins. However, even in modern conditions, this urban elite depends upon others who do not belong to it: the farmers, manufacturers, factory workers, builders, clothiers, mechanics, nurses, carers, cleaners, cooks, policemen and soldiers for whom attachment to a place and its customs is implicit in all that they do. In a question that touches on identity, these people will very likely vote in another way from the urban elite, on whom they depend in turn for government.

It seems, then, that the word 'we' in this context does not always embrace the same group of people or the same networks of association. David Goodhart has presented a dichotomy between the 'anywheres' and the 'somewheres', those who can take their business, their relations and their networks from place to place without detriment, and those for whom a specific place and its indigenous lifestyle are woven into their social being.[1] These two kinds of people will be pulled in different directions when asked to consider what really holds their community together. According to Goodhart, 'the people from Anywhere in Britain – including the metropolitan elites of left and right, reflecting the interests of the upper professional class – have dominated the political agenda whichever party has been in power for the past twenty-five years and have too often failed to distinguish their

[1] David Goodhart, *The Road to Somewhere: The Populist Revolt and the Future of Politics*, London, 2017.

own sectional interests from the general interest'.[2] And Goodhart's book is a delicate and well-argued plea for the 'somewheres', whose interests have been neglected in recent political decisions, and who sent a message of 'Leave' to the politicians in the Brexit vote.

However, it is surely apparent to all of us that we are in need of an inclusive first-person plural, one that unites both the mobile elite and the settled people. The identities of earlier periods – dynasty, faith, family, tribe – were already weakening when the Enlightenment began the process of consigning them to oblivion. And the substitute identities of more recent times – the ideologies and the 'isms' of the totalitarian states – have transparently failed to provide an alternative. But the British have enjoyed throughout the modern era another kind of identity entirely, one that has depended neither on doctrine nor national myth, but simply on the customs and institutions that have made us live together in a condition of mutual responsibility.

We in Britain are officially 'subjects of the Queen', not citizens, and the distinction is an important one. The word 'citizen' was used at the American and French Revolutions in order to denote the new status of the individual as an autonomous member of society, owing no obedience to a monarch. The term was used in France

[2] ibid., p. 10.

as an everyday title and form of address, though retaining the ideological overtones satirized by Flaubert in *L'Éducation sentimentale*. Today it denotes a condition distinct from both American citizenship and British subjecthood. The French citizen is bound to the state in a legal relation in which it has the upper hand. The state is aggressively secular, imposing a rule of *laïcité* that forbids citizens openly to wear religious symbols or to dilute their citizenship with religious forms of obedience. The *citoyen* is, in many respects, the property of *L'État*, and his house can be invaded and rifled by the police or the tax inspectors without any proof of wrongdoing.

The British subject, by contrast, is bound to the Queen by a loose bond of affection, which has few precise terms. We also have a secular government, but not an *aggressively* secular government, since the Queen is also head of a national Church, the Bishops of which sit in Parliament. There are other important differences too, as I point out in Chapter Five, and these differences are part of what we might have in mind in distinguishing the British subject from the French citizen. However, it is appropriate to use the terms 'subject' and 'citizen' in a more general sense, according to which both the French and the British are citizens of their countries. Citizenship in this broader sense consists of a web of reciprocal rights and duties, upheld by a rule of law to which both the state and the citizen must submit.

Although the state enforces the law, therefore, it administers it equally against itself and against the private citizen. The citizen has rights that the state is duty-bound to uphold, and also duties that the state has a right to enforce. Because these rights and duties are defined and limited by the law, citizens have a clear conception of where their freedoms end. Where citizens are appointed to administer the state, the result is 'republican' government.[3] And citizenship has been the most evident gift of the modern nation state, in which people accept a territorial definition of membership in place of the religious and dynastic definitions that had led to the conflicts which tore Europe apart at the Reformation. In this sense the 'subjects' of our Queen are also citizens, and in some respects more obviously citizens than many other European nationals.

This does not mean that all nation states are composed of citizens. In several of the nation states that emerged from the Peace of Westphalia in 1648 the people were not citizens but subjects, in the traditional understanding of that term. Subjection is the relation between the state and the individual that arises when the state need

[3] I adopt this definition in order to identify an ideal that has been defended in various forms by Aristotle, Machiavelli, Montesquieu, Kant and the American Founding Fathers. Republican government is not to be contrasted with monarchy (our own government is both), but with absolute rule, dictatorship, one-party rule, and a host of other possibilities that fall short of participatory administration. Nor are republican governments necessarily democratic.

not account to the individual, when the rights and duties of the individual are undefined or defined only partially and subject to erasure, and when there is no rule of law that stands higher than the state. Citizens are freer than subjects, not because there is more that they can get away with, but because their freedoms are defined and upheld by the law. People who are subjects naturally aspire to be citizens, since citizens can take definite steps to secure their property, family and business against marauders, and have effective sovereignty over their own lives. That is why people migrate from the countries where they are subjects to the countries where they can be citizens.

Freedom and security are not the only benefits of citizenship. There is an economic benefit too. Under a rule of law contracts can be freely engaged in and collectively enforced. Honesty becomes the rule in business dealings, and disputes are settled by courts of law rather than by hired thugs. And because the principle of accountability runs through all institutions, corruption can be identified and penalized, even when it occurs at the highest level of government. That is another reason why people migrate to places where they can enjoy the benefit of citizenship. A society of citizens is one in which markets flourish, and there are opportunities open to the newcomer.

A society of citizens is a society in which everyone is bound by a common set of rules. This does not mean that there are no thieves or swindlers; it means that trust can grow between strangers, and does not depend upon family connections, tribal loyalties or favours granted and earned. This strikingly distinguishes a country such as Australia, for example, from a country like Kazakhstan, where the economy depends on the mutual exchange of favours, among people who trust each other only because they also know each other and know the networks that will be used to enforce any deal.[4] It is also why Australia has an immigration problem, and Kazakhstan a brain drain.

As a result of this, trust among citizens can spread over a wide area, and local baronies and fiefdoms can be broken down and overruled. In such circumstances markets do not merely flourish: they spread and grow, to become co-extensive with the jurisdiction. Every citizen becomes linked to every other, by relations that are financial, legal and fiduciary, but which presuppose no personal tie. A society of citizens can be a society of strangers, all enjoying sovereignty over their own lives, and pursuing their individual goals and satisfactions. Such are Western societies today. They are societies in which you form common cause with strangers, and in which all of you, in those matters on which your common destiny depends, can with conviction say 'we'.

---

[4] See Francis Fukuyama, *Trust: The Social Virtues and the Creation of Prosperity*, New York, 1995.

The existence of this kind of trust in a society of strangers should be seen for what it is: a rare achievement, whose preconditions are not easily fulfilled. If it is difficult for us to appreciate this fact, it is in part because trust between strangers creates an illusion of safety, encouraging people to think that, because society ends in agreement, it begins in agreement too. Thus it has been normal since the Renaissance for thinkers to propose some version of the 'social contract' as the foundation of a society of citizens. But if people are in a position to decide in this way on their common future, it is because they already have one: because they recognize their mutual togetherness and reciprocal dependence, which makes it incumbent upon them to settle how they might be governed under a common jurisdiction in a common territory. Philosophers of the social contract write as though it presupposes only the first-person singular of free rational choice. In fact it presupposes a first-person plural, in which the burdens of belonging have already been assumed. Hence, in the immediate aftermath of the Reformation, British people, both English and Scots, often described themselves as bound by a 'covenant'. The term invokes the bond between the Israelites and their God – a bond that preceded, in time and in essence, any specific duty of the parties.

It is because citizenship presupposes membership that nationality has become so important in the modern world. Nationality is not the only kind of pre-political membership, nor is it an exclusive tie. However, it is the only form of membership that has shown itself able to sustain a democratic process and a liberal rule of law. We should compare communities defined by nationhood with those defined by tribe or creed. Tribal societies define themselves through a fiction of kinship. The people see themselves as members of an extended family, and even if they are strangers, this fact is only superficial, to be instantly put aside on discovery of the common ancestor and the common web of kin. Tribal societies tend to be hierarchical, with accountability running one way – from subject to chief, but not from chief to subject. The idea of an impartial rule of law, sustained in being by the very government that is subject to it, has no place in the world of kinship ties, and when it comes to outsiders – the 'strangers and sojourners' in the land of the tribe – they are regarded either as outside the law altogether and not entitled to its protection, or as protected by treaty.[5] Nor can outsiders easily become insiders, since that which divides them from the tribe is an irredeemable genetic fault.

Distinct from the tribe, but closely connected with it, is the 'creed community' – the society whose criterion of

---

[5] Such is the concept of the *dhimma* in Islamic law. See Antoine Fattal, *Le statut légal des non-Musulmans en pays d'Islam*, Beirut, 1958.

membership is religious. I am joined to those who worship my gods, and accept the same divine prescriptions, even though we are strangers. Creed communities, like tribes, extend their claims beyond the living. The dead acquire the privileges of the worshipper through the latter's prayers. But the dead are present in the ceremonies on very different terms. They no longer have the authority of tribal ancestors; rather, they are subjects of the same divine overlord, undergoing their reward or punishment in conditions of greater proximity to the ruling power. They throng together in the great unknown, just as we will, released from every earthly tie and united by faith.[6]

The initial harmony between tribal and religious criteria of membership may give way to conflict, as the rival forces of family loyalty and religious obedience exert themselves over small communities. This conflict has been one of the motors of Islamic history, forms the background to the pacification offered in the Koran, and can be witnessed all over the Middle East, where local creed communities have grown out of the monotheistic religions and shaped themselves according to a tribal experience of membership.

It is in contrast with the tribal and religious forms of membership that the nation should be understood. By a

---

[6] I take the term 'creed community' from Spengler, and discuss what it means in *The West and the Rest*, London, 2002.

nation I mean a people settled in a certain territory, who share language, institutions, customs and a sense of history, and who regard themselves as equally committed both to their place of residence and to the legal and political processes that govern it. Members of tribes see each other as a family; members of creed communities see each other as the faithful; members of nations see each other as neighbours. Vital to the sense of nationhood, therefore, is the idea of a common territory, to which we are all entitled as our home. This sense of entitlement does not depend on residence: it is often stronger in those who travel far from home on personal or official business, or who reside in some other country. But its foundation is a vision of peace among neighbours, in a home that they share.

People who share a territory share a history; they may also share a language and a religion. The European nation state emerged when this idea of a community defined by a place was enshrined in sovereignty and law – in other words when it was aligned with a territorial jurisdiction. The nation state is therefore the natural successor to territorial monarchy, and the two may be combined, and often have been combined, since the monarch is so convenient a symbol of the trans-generational ties that bind us to our country.

The theory that the nation is a recent invention, the creation of the modern administrative state, was probably first articulated by Lord Acton in a thin but celebrated article.[7] Writers from all parts of the political spectrum seem to endorse versions of this view, arguing that nations are bureaucratic inventions, whose emergence is inseparable from the culture of the written word.[8] Radicals use this fact to suggest that nations are transient, with no natural legitimacy, while conservatives use it to suggest the opposite, that nationality is an achievement, a 'winning through' to an order that is both more stable and more open than the religious and tribal atavisms that it replaces.

When it is said that nations are artificial communities, however, it should be remembered that there are two kinds of social artefact: those that result from a decision, as when two people form a partnership, and those that arise 'by an invisible hand', from decisions that in no way intend them, such as folk songs and folk religions. Institutions that arise by an invisible hand have a spontaneity and naturalness that may be lacking from institutions that are explicitly designed. Nations are spontaneous byproducts of social interaction. Even when there is a conscious nation-building decision, the result will depend on the invisible hand: it is the affection, not the decision, that shapes the national identity. This is even true

[7] J. E. E. Dalberg-Acton, first Baron Acton, 'Nationality', in *The History of Freedom and Other Essays*, ed. J. N. Figgis and R. V. Lawrence, London, 1907.

[8] Ernest Gellner, *Nations and Nationalism*, Oxford, 1983; Benedict Anderson, *Imagined Communities*, 2nd edn, London, 1991; Eric Hobsbawm, *Nations and Nationalism since 1780*, Cambridge, 1990; Elie Kedourie, *Nationalism*, London, 1960; Kenneth Minogue, *Nationalism*, London, 1967.

of the United States of America, which is by no means the entity today that the Founding Fathers intended. Yet the USA is one of the most vital and most patriotic nations in the modern world, and the final destination for a vast number of migrants eager to exchange the condition of the subject for that of the citizen.

The example also illustrates Lord Acton's thesis. Nations are composed of neighbours, in other words of people who share a territory. Hence they stand in need of a territorial jurisdiction. Territorial jurisdictions require courts, legislation and a political process. This process transforms shared territory into a shared identity. And that identity is the nation state. There you have a brief summary of American history: people settling together, solving their conflicts by law, making that law for themselves, and in the course of this process defining themselves as a 'we', whose shared assets are the land and its law.

The 'invisible hand' process, which was so illuminatingly discussed by Adam Smith, depends upon, and is secretly guided by, a legal and institutional framework.[9] Under a rule of law, for example, the free interaction of individuals will result in a market economy. In the legal

---

[9] See Adam Smith, *Inquiry into the Nature and the Causes of the Wealth of Nations*, 1776, and the discussion of 'invisible hand' explanations in Robert Nozick, *Anarchy, State and Utopia*, Oxford, 1974. The invisible-hand theory was generalized by F. A. Hayek to produce a comprehensive account of legal and institutional development, in *Law, Legislation and Liberty*, 2 vols, London, 1976.

vacuum of post-communist Russia, by contrast, this free interaction of individuals has produced a command economy in the hands of gangsters. Likewise the invisible hand that gave rise to the nation was guided at every point by the territorial law. This 'law of the land' has been an important shaping force in English history, as F. W. Maitland and others have shown. [10] And it is through the process whereby land and law become attached to each other that our specific form of national allegiance has been formed.

People cannot share territory without sharing many other things too: language, customs, markets and (in European conditions) religion. Hence every territorial jurisdiction will be associated with complex and interlocking loyalties of a religious and dynastic kind. However, it will also seek to change those loyalties. Territorial law treats individuals as bearers of rights and duties. It recasts their relations with their neighbours in abstract terms; it shows a preference for contract over status and for definable interests over inarticulate bonds. It is hostile to all power and authority that is not exerted from within the jurisdiction. In short, it imprints on the community a distinctive political form. Hence, when the English nation took shape in the Middle Ages, it became inevitable that the English would have a Church of their

[10] F. W. Maitland, *The Constitutional History of England*, London, 1908.

own, and that their faith would be defined by their allegiance, rather than their allegiance by their faith. In making himself head of the Church of England, Henry VIII was translating into a doctrine of law (though against considerable resistance) what was already a matter of fact.

At the same time, we must not think of territorial jurisdiction as merely a conventional arrangement: a kind of ongoing and severable agreement, of the kind that appealed to the Social Contract thinkers of the Enlightenment. It involves a genuine 'we' of membership: not as visceral as that of kinship; not as uplifting as that of worship, but for those very reasons more suited to the modern world and to a society in which faith is dwindling or dead. It is the paradigm case of a society held together by trust between strangers, who may have nothing in common, save the place where they are and the customs that have arisen there.

A settled jurisdiction, defined by territory, has established from Saxon times a reciprocal accountability between 'us' and the sovereign who is 'ours'. The result of this has been an experience of safety, quite different from that of the tribe, but connected with the shared place to which we belong. The common language – itself the product of territorial settlement – has reinforced the feeling. But to suppose that we could have enjoyed these territorial, legal and linguistic legacies, and yet refrained from becoming a nation, representing itself to itself as entitled to these things, and defining even its religion in terms of them, is to give way to fantasy. In no way can the emergence of our nation, as a form of membership, be regarded as a product of Enlightenment universalism, or the Industrial Revolution, or the administrative needs of a modern bureaucracy. It existed before those things, shaped them into powerful instruments of its own and was in turn shaped by them. Moreover, when, in due course, the dynastic and religious conflicts were settled, it became all but inevitable that England would become part of a 'union', in which Wales was already assumed as a member, while Scotland and Ireland were one after the other brought under a single political process. We could describe the result as four nations contained within a single state, or equally as a nation state with four component parts. We are not describing eternal and immutable fusions, but *settlements*, arrangements whereby people have come to coexist in a shared territory and to accept the customs and loyalties that divide them in the interest of those other customs and institutions whereby they are united in a single body politic. Such arrangements are malleable, but intrinsically self-legitimizing, notwithstanding G. K. Chesterton's attempt, in *The Napoleon of Notting Hill*, to dismiss territorial identities as arbitrary.

To put the matter simply: nations are defined not by kinship or religion but by a homeland. Europe owes its greatness to the fact that the primary loyalties of the European people have been detached from religion and attached instead to the land. Those who believe that the division of Europe into nations has been the primary cause of European wars should remember the devastating wars of religion that national loyalties finally brought to an end. And they should study our art and literature, which is an art and literature not of war but of peace, an invocation of home and the routines of home, of everydayness and enduring settlement. Its quarrels are domestic quarrels, its protests are pleas for neighbours, its goal is homecoming and contentment with the place that is ours.¹¹ Even the popular culture of the modern world is a covert reaffirmation of a territorial form of loyalty. *The Archers*, *Neighbours*, *Coronation Street*, *East Enders*: all such mirrors of ordinary existence are in the business of showing settlement and neighbourhood, rather than tribe or religion, as the primary social legacies. And similar celebrations of everyday togetherness occur in every jurisdiction – in European democracies (the French *Plus belle la vie*), in autocratic Arab states (the *musalsalat* broadcast each evening in Ramadan), or in the many Latin American countries addicted to the *telenovela*. Even in places ruled by religious, tribal or

---

¹¹ A few classic instances: George Eliot, *Middlemarch*; Adalbert Stifter, *Nachsommer*; Marcel Proust, *À la recherche du temps perdu*; Ingmar Bergman, *Wild Strawberries*; James Joyce, *Dubliners*. And so on.

sectarian dictatorship, the human heart tends towards place, family and neighbourhood as its source of belonging. The European achievement is to have transcribed that feeling into politics and law.

The first-person plural of nationhood, unlike those of tribe or religion, is intrinsically tolerant of difference.[12] It involves a respect for privacy, and a desire for citizenship, in which people maintain sovereignty over their own lives and the kind of distance that makes such sovereignty possible. The 'clash of civilizations', which, according to Samuel Huntington, is the successor to the Cold War is, in my view, no such thing. It is a conflict between two forms of membership – the national, which tolerates difference, and the religious, which does not.[13] It is this toleration of difference that opens the way to democracy, and every move beyond the nation state, towards some transnational centre of government, is a move away from democracy. That is what those who voted to leave the European Union largely perceived, and the point was emphasized by the unelected head of the European Commission, Jean-Claude Juncker, when

[12] See Scruton, *The West and the Rest*, op. cit. See also Jonathan Sacks, *The Dignity of Difference*, London, 2002, in which the former Chief Rabbi defends the respect for cultural and religious difference that the nation state makes possible, and which vanishes when the only form of available membership is religious or tribal.

[13] Samuel Huntington, *The Clash of Civilizations and the Remaking of World Order*, New York, 1996.

he remarked that 'there can be no democratic choice against the European Treaties'.[14]

Patriotism involves a love of home and a preparedness to defend it; nationalism, by contrast, is a belligerent *ideology*, which uses national symbols in order to conscript the people to war. When the Abbé Sieyès declared the aims of the French Revolution, it was in the language of nationalism: 'The nation is prior to everything. It is the source of everything. Its will is always legal . . . The manner in which a nation exercises its will does not matter; the point is that it does exercise it; any procedure is adequate, and its will is always the supreme law.'[15] Those words express the very opposite of a true national loyalty. Not only do they involve an idolatrous deification of the 'Nation', elevating it far above the people of whom it is in fact composed. They do so in order to punish, to exclude, to threaten rather than to facilitate citizenship and to guarantee peace. The nation is here being deified, and used to intimidate its members, to purge the common home of those who are thought to pollute it. And the way is being prepared for the abolition of all legal restraint, and the destruction of the territorial rule of law. In short, this kind of nationalism is not a national

---

[14] *Le Figaro*, 28 January 2016.

[15] E. Sieyès, *What Is the Third Estate?*, tr. M. Blondel, ed. S. E. Finer, London, 1963, pp. 124, 128.

loyalty, but a religious loyalty dressed up in territorial clothes.[16]

There is already in the social contract theories of the eighteenth century a kind of wishful thinking about human nature, a belief that people can reshape their obligations without reference to their affections, so as to produce an abstract calculus of rights and duties in the place of their contingent and historical ties. The French Revolutionaries began their seizure of power by proposing a 'Declaration of the Rights of Man and of the Citizen' that would sweep away all the arbitrary arrangements of history, so as to place Reason on the throne that had previously been occupied by a mere human being. But within weeks of the Declaration, while the country was being governed in the name of the Nation, the *Patrie*, and the Rights of Man, the old contingent association was being summoned in another and far more dangerous form, in order to fill the gap in people's affections that had been made by the destruction of custom and neighbourhood. Very soon it became clear that the 'rights' promised in the Declaration had not been conferred on the 'enemies of the people', that those enemies were everywhere and that no citizen could be sure that he wasn't one of them.

---

[16] On the tendency of nationalism to degenerate into a combative religion see Adam Zamoyski, *Holy Madness: Romantics, Patriots and Revolutionaries*, London, 1999.

This was clearly perceived by Edmund Burke, who reminded his readers that human beings are thrown together by accidents that they do not choose, and derive their affections not from their decisions but from their circumstances.[17] It is proximity, not reason, that is the foundation of ordinary charitable feeling. Take that thought seriously, and you quickly come to see that territorial forms of association are the best remedy that we have against the divisive call of ideology. National loyalty, construed as the low-key patriotism of custom and place, is precisely what prevents 'extremism' from taking hold of the ordinary conscience. It is at the root of all that is best in human society, namely that we are attached to what goes on around us, grow together with it, and learn the ways of peaceful association as *our* ways, which are right because they are ours and because they unite us with those who came before us and those who will replace us in our turn. Seen in that way patriotic feelings are not just natural, they are essentially *legitimizing*. They call upon the sources of social affection, and bestow that affection on customs that have proved their worth over time, by enabling a community to settle its disputes and achieve equilibrium in the changing circumstances of life. All this was expressed by Ernest Renan, in his celebrated essay of 1882, *Qu'est-ce qu'une*

[17] Edmund Burke, *Reflections on the Revolution in France*, 1791.

nation?[18] For Renan a nation is not constituted by racial or religious conformity, but by a 'daily plebiscite', expressing the collective memory of the members, and their present consent to live together. It is precisely for these reasons that national sentiments open the way to democratic politics.

It is because we are able to define our membership in territorial terms that we, in Western countries, enjoy the elementary freedoms that are, for us, the foundation of political order. In states such as Iran and Saudi Arabia, founded on religious rather than territorial obedience, freedom of conscience is a scarce and threatened asset. (In Iran the mere possession of the New Testament is seriously risky.) We, however, enjoy not merely the freedom publicly to disagree with others about matters of faith and private life, but also the freedom to satirize solemnity and to ridicule nonsense, including solemnity and nonsense of the religious kind. All such freedoms are precious to us, and are bound together with our sense of being the heirs to a shared form of life, and an unspoken way of doing things that we can easily recognize, though not so easily describe.

As I have already noted, we British do not, in fact, define our shared identity in the explicitly national terms spelled out by Renan. We belong to a complex political

[18] Ernest Renan, *Qu'est-ce qu'une nation?*, lecture at the Sorbonne, 11 March 1882.

organism, comprising three and a half nations – the English, the Scots, the Welsh and a large section of the Irish – who have migrated freely between their territories over many centuries of negotiation and conflict. Similar stories can be told of other countries too, and one thing that is wrong with the ideological form of nationalism is the belief that people owe political loyalty primarily to their kith and kin, rather than to their neighbours. It is true that our present crisis of identity is the result of unprecedented waves of immigration. But it should not be forgotten that migration has proceeded apace from the beginning of history, and is largely what history consists in. Borders dissolve or are overrun, languages mingle and amalgamate, religions split into divergent and mutually hostile sects. In every arrangement people cling to old definitions of identity for fear of losing what is most precious to them, which is the trust on which they depend for survival.

The crucial thing is not that we can avail ourselves of some eternal community, with fixed borders, unalterable beliefs and a ring-fenced genetic inheritance. What is crucial is that, in the flow of human fortunes, there should be a place of belonging, which we can identify as our home, where the inhabitants can be relied upon, and which we are all committed to defending and improving for the common good. It is crucial too that our home be governed by institutions to which we tacitly subscribe – a law-making and law-enforcing process on which we can rely in the settlement of disputes and in which our many interests are represented. This is the residual idea of national identity that I defend in this book – the idea of a shared home and a territorial jurisdiction. It is neither belligerent nor mystical, and does not depend upon extinguishing the many other loyalties that its participants may have.

In Goodhart's language, it is as possible for the 'anywheres' as it is for the 'somewheres' to identify their allegiance in national terms. You can be a loyal subject of the British Crown, and also English, Scottish, Irish or Welsh when it comes to other aspects of belonging. You can be a British Nigerian or a British Pakistani, and the future of our country depends upon the process of integration that will persuade new arrivals that this is not only possible, but also the true promise that our country offers. It is possible to be a British Muslim, in the manner of Sara Khan, as much as a British Jew or Christian.[19] Nationality, defined by borders, land and sovereignty, does not extinguish local loyalties, or the residue of older and more rooted ties. It is not opposed to transnational cooperation, or to patriotic feelings towards countries that are not one's own. Everything here is a matter of

[19] See in particular Sara Khan's book with Tony McMahon, *The Battle for British Islam: Reclaiming Muslim Identity from Extremism*, London, 2016.

degree, tempered by the ongoing negotiation between neighbours that is the stuff of a free democracy.

Of course those other loyalties may seek to establish territorial jurisdictions of their own, and this is now routine in Europe, partly because the European Union has disrupted old forms of identity while providing no real replacement for them. It could be, therefore, that Scotland will become an independent sovereign state, and that Scottish national feeling will give rise to a political order of its own. If this happens it will not be by violence, but in the manner of the divorce between the Czech Republic and Slovakia, in which a shared home was divided by agreement, and all other loyalties remained intact. Whether it should happen and, if not, whether there is a way to prevent it, are questions that I address in the final chapter.

There is another and deeper reason for adhering to the nation as the source of legal obligation. Only when the law derives from national sovereignty or some comparable idea of territorial legitimacy can it adapt to the changing conditions of the people. We see this clearly in the futile attempt of modern Islamic states to live by the shari'ah. When the clerics take over, law is referred back to precepts designed for the government of a long since vanished community, riven by tribal warfare in the Arabian Desert, but brought to order by Muhammad with a series of recitations that purported to lay down

God's commandments as law. Jurists have great difficulty in adapting such a law to the life of modern people.
Secular law adapts, but religious law endures. Moreover,
precisely because the shari'ah has not adapted, nobody
really knows what it says. Does it tell us that investing
money at interest is in every case forbidden? Some say
yes, some say no.[20] Does it tell us to punish thieves by
mutilation and homosexuals and adulterers by stoning to
death? Some say yes, some say no. When God makes the
laws, the laws become as mysterious as God is. When *we*
make the laws, and make them for our purposes, we can
be certain what they mean. The question then is 'who
are *we*?' In particular, what way of defining ourselves is
compatible with a democratic process, and popular sovereignty? The nation is one tried and proven answer to
that question.

Laws laid down by God have the eternal and changeless character of their author. But the same defect attends
laws laid down by a treaty. Treaties are dead hands, which
should be laid upon a country only for specific and essential purposes, and never as a way of governing them.
Thus, when the Treaty of Rome was signed in 1957 it
included a clause permitting the free movement of
capital and labour between the signatories. At the time
incomes and opportunities were roughly similar across

[20] See Nabil Saleh, *Unlawful Gain and Legitimate Profit in Islamic Law*, Oxford, 1986.

the small number of states that signed, and economists theorized the market in terms of the free deployment of the 'factors of production', of which capital and labour were two. Now things are very different. Not only has economics proceeded on its vacillating course from that particular theory to the next one, but the movement of people has become one of the major problems confronting all European states, both those that are gaining people and those that are losing them.

In one sense the 'free movement of labour' has been a long-standing principle in British foreign relations. So long as someone has an offer of employment in Britain, and so long as the employer can make out a case that this is the right person for the job, it has been normal to grant a right of residence, for as long as the job endures. When Britain joined the European Economic Community, as it then was, the provision in the Treaty was explained in those terms, and the government of Mr Heath saw no problem in signing up to it.

However, this is not how the 'free movement' clause is now interpreted. The Treaty of Maastricht created a new constitutional status: 'citizenship of the European Union'. This status bestows entitlements, enforceable by the European Court of Justice, including the right to reside anywhere in the EU, whether or not to take up an offer of a job, the right to vote in local and European elections, and the right to non-discrimination on grounds of nationality. This last right has been widely interpreted (as was the intention) to mean equal access to benefits, subsidized university places, social housing and healthcare.

Hence the 'free movement of labour' now means the 'free movement of people', even those who move without the offer of a job, and whose freedom to move involves a claim for benefits, education and social housing. The European Union has expanded to include most of the countries of Eastern Europe, countries ruined by communism, whose citizens now have the legal right to take up residence within our national borders, seeking jobs, housing, benefits and healthcare, and fundamentally altering the social fabric of many cities and the makeup of their schools. True, scare-stories in the popular press about 'benefits tourism' are exaggerated, and appeal to ungenerous sentiments: probably only 2 per cent of those claiming the full range of benefits in 2011 were nationals of the former communist countries.[21] Nevertheless, around 70,000 EU citizens a year enter the kingdom without any offer of employment here, and at a time of acute housing shortage and traumatic changes in employment patterns many British citizens are unhappy with this situation, which has led to an addition to our population of over 2 million residents in a

[21] See the report issued by the Department of Work and Pensions in January 2012: 'Nationality at point of National Insurance number registration of DWP benefit claims', on the government website.

decade. But because the law permitting it was inscribed within a treaty, and the interpretation of the treaty was vested in an extraterritorial court that claims sovereignty over our Parliament, there is nothing that can be done about it, short of Brexit. It is just as though we too have been governed by a kind of religious law, in which the will of God sounds through every edict, preventing even the most necessary change.

I mention the 'free movement of people' here, not because it was the most important consideration in the minds of those who voted for Brexit – according to the poll taken by Lord Ashcroft on the day of the vote it was far less important than the issue of sovereignty – but because it is so clearly a matter about which each nation should have the right to make up its mind.[22] Population movements change rapidly and in response to unforeseeable circumstances (such as the sudden collapse of communism in Eastern Europe). To be deprived of the legal and political instruments whereby to adapt to these changes is to have lost what is most important in democratic government. It is only fair to add that the government of Tony Blair exacerbated the problem, by opening the British labour market in 2004 to workers from the new East European member states, seven years before

---

[22] Ashcroft's survey is reported in Daniel Hannan, *What Next?*, London, 2017.

the EU required this. In the next chapter I offer a partial explanation for this catastrophic decision.

It is national attachment, I contend, that has made citizenship possible, and enabled people to exist side by side, respecting each other's rights, despite radical differences in faith, and without any bonds of family, kinship or long-term local custom to sustain the solidarity between them. Nor has the EU really changed this. The French are still united by a 'daily plebiscite' of Renan's kind, just as the Germans and the Spaniards are. And most Europeans appreciate the gift of nationality, even if they have no theory to explain it, and even if the Germans are understandably screwed up about it. In a society of citizens it is possible to establish good relations and a shared allegiance among strangers. You don't have to know your fellow citizens in order to ascertain your rights or your duties towards them, and their being strangers, dissenters, heretics or weirdos in no way alters the fact that you are each prepared to defend the territory that includes you. This remarkable feature of citizen-states was praised as the ruling principle of Athenian democracy by Pericles, in the funeral oration attributed to him by Thucydides. What the Islamist movements promise to their adherents is not citizenship but *brotherhood* — *ikhwān* — an altogether warmer, closer and more metaphysically satisfying relation, but one that is quickly inflamed by any real difference of opinion.

We should therefore take a lesson from the fragility of political order in the Islamic world, not least because it is refugees from that world who are now most actively challenging political order in the West. We should recognize that, by defining our basic allegiance in national terms, we have secured ourselves against the worst of civil conflicts, and also provided the first-person plural with which to address the wider world. If we ask ourselves who we are, then we have a ready and poignant answer, which indicates our determination to stay together in a perpetual 'agreement to differ'. We belong to this place, *our country*, and this country defines us. And if we extend a welcome to newcomers, then we must be clear that we are inviting them to belong here in the same way that we do. It is citizenship that we offer them: not the rights of citizenship only, but the duties too. And these rights and duties belong to the place where we are.

4

OUR COUNTRY: RIGHT
OR WRONG

Whatever narrative of the past we adhere to, we accept it because it tells us what we are *now*. And it can do this in one of two ways: by telling us either that we are just as good as we have always been, or that we are no longer the bad people we once were. The second, negative, perspective has been taught in our schools for a long time now, and it is not surprising, therefore, if young people today find it harder to identify themselves with their country than those of us who grew up in the immediate post-war decades.

Historical narratives do not owe their power to their truth, but to the 'will to believe'. They exist in the same psychic sphere as myths and religions – embellishments to life that grow from what we do and what we feel and not from what we rationally think. I believe in the positive narrative of our past, and find abundant proof of it in the powerfully argued summary given by Robert Tombs in *The English and Their History*.[1] But I know that

---

[1] Robert Tombs, *The English and their History*, London, 2014.

many of my contemporaries do not accept that narrative. Moreover, it is precisely the patriotic commitment of the sceptics that is now most needed.

Among educated people various factors have exacerbated the negative feelings towards our past. There is the growing 'culture of repudiation' that we witness in the public channels of communication; there is the connected ethic of 'non-discrimination', arising in response to a widespread sense that we are not entitled to our inherited advantages. And there is the narrative of national decline, which tells us that, whatever greatness and strength we once possessed, the story now is one of weakness, incompetence and fragmentation. All three accusations avoid comparative judgements. And this is already significant, a proof that our most radical critics speak from within, covertly accepting the context of a shared home. As in family quarrels, comparisons have no part to play: what family quarrel has ended with the question, 'Compared with which father am I such a tyrant?'

It is important to understand the accusations nevertheless, since our response to them critically affects the future of our country, and indeed the future of all countries in the tenuous but persisting alliance that unites the Western democracies. However unjustified the negative attitudes may be, they cannot be dismissed as fashions, since they do not arise from any conscious rivalry or social posturing. Nor are they the result of reasoned argument, as is shown precisely by the lack of comparative judgements. There may be such an argument, of course. But argument and fashion are both of small significance in assessing postures of affirmation or denial. These postures come into being as 'gut reactions' – stances towards the social world that originate in those parts of the psyche that can be more easily explained than altered, and which colour all our thoughts and decisions regardless of our ability to support them with persuasive reasoning.

The need for home is an adaptation, which generates motives that can be witnessed in every aspect of a settled life. In his three great studies of children – *Attachment*, *Separation* and *Loss* – John Bowlby provides overwhelming evidence for the view that interpersonal love and relational competence are rooted in an original experience of attachment, that children deprived of that experience are disturbed and often profoundly asocial, and that both normal adult relations and the capacity for love are critically dependent on the core experience of home.[2] The evidence abounds that home is not merely 'where we start from', but the place that we hope to rediscover, albeit in a form adapted to our adult personality. It has this status in our self-conscious feelings, which feed

[2] John Bowlby, *Attachment*, *Separation* and *Loss*, 3 vols, New York, 1999–2001.

upon those primeval adaptations, but it grows in time to embrace all our projects.

Those observations establish, to my mind without question, that human beings, in their settled condition, are animated by the attitude that I call oikophilia: the love of the *oikos*, which means not only the home but the people contained in it, and the surrounding settlements that endow that home with its personality. The *oikos* is the place that is not just mine and yours but ours. It is the stage-set for the first-person plural of politics, the locus, both real and imagined, where it all 'takes place'.

At the same time growing children experience a countervailing force: a vector towards detachment, which becomes stronger in the years of adolescence and which leads, or ought to lead, to a move away from the original home towards a home of their own. The adolescent consents to love the home and its occupants, yes, but not to be trapped by them, as though trapped for life. It is this necessary experience of detachment that may transmute into a posture of repudiation, coloured by the distinguishing mark of all gut reactions that stem from the family, which is guilt.

Nobody brought up in our country since the Second World War can fail to be aware of this guilt, which makes it all but impossible either to confess to our original attachments, or to speak of them without a measure of scepticism. A quantity of educated derision has been directed towards historical loyalties by our intellectual elites, who regularly dismiss the ordinary forms of patriotic sentiment as racism, imperialism or xenophobia. I coin the term oikophobia to denote this attitude, on the analogy of the xenophobia of which it accuses our inherited way of life. I do not mean the *fear* of home, however, but the repudiation of home – the turning away from the inherited first-person plural.

Oikophobia is a stage through which the adolescent mind all but inevitably passes. But it is also a stage in which we can become arrested. Orwell noticed this in the English intellectuals of his day, but it is not a specifically British phenomenon. When Sartre and Foucault draw their picture of the 'bourgeois' mentality, the mentality of the Others in their Otherness, they are describing the ordinary decent French citizen, and expressing their contempt for the national culture. This contempt was for a while the dominant theme of French intellectual life, to be found in all the post-1968 nonsense, from Luce Irigaray to Hélène Cixous, and from Gilles Deleuze to Julia Kristeva, that has spread from the *rive gauche* to humanities departments around the world.

This returns me again to David Goodhart's distinction between the 'somewheres' and the 'anywheres'. There are those for whom the attachment to a specific place and the form of life that grows there is definitive of their condition, and who wish at all costs to conserve that place as the home to which they belong. And there are those who are easily uprooted, can take their skills and their social networks effortlessly from place to place, and generally find the niche in which to settle. Education, imagination and skills will endow people with this 'anywhere' character, whereas those who lack such advantages will be more tenacious of the habits that they know. In Britain, where a half of adolescents attend university, and university generally involves a move away from home, the young increasingly acquire an 'anywhere' identity: hence their shift to the left in recent elections.

The European Union, with its commitment to freedom of movement and its hostility to the 'nationalist' sentiments of ordinary people, is likewise an 'anywhere' project, which confers benefits on the mobile and costs on the settled communities that must make room for them. But both kinds of person can in the course of time develop attachments. Oikophilia is the common property of all who wish to settle down, and the anywheres will, in time, give in to it. That is how great cities are created, when the anywheres hit on a somewhere of their own. Opinion polls have suggested that both sides in the Brexit debate – the leavers and the remainers – identify what matters most to them as job, family and place, in other words, as the three normal ways of being rooted.[3]

[3] Surveys conducted by BMG research on behalf of the Commission for National Renewal.

It is not Goodhart's distinction that I have in mind, therefore, in contrasting oikophilia and oikophobia. From
Byron to Orwell the great literary wanderers have written in praise of rooted communities and the charmed
places that sustain them. Anywheres find meaning in the
somewheres that others create, as Byron found meaning
in Venice and Orwell in the industrial communities on
the road to Wigan Pier. The wanderings of an anywhere
person are invoked in *Childe Harold's Pilgrimage* – trav-
els among shrines, each made holy by the people who
live there.

The roots of oikophobia lie elsewhere than in the
desire to be elsewhere. Indeed they lie deeper than reason, and it is unlikely that any argument will eradicate
them. Oikophobes define their goals and ideals *against*
some cherished form of membership – against the family, the nation, indeed against anything that makes a
claim, however justified, on their loyalty. They promote
transnational institutions over national governments,
defining their political vision in terms of universal values
that have been purged of all reference to the particular
attachments of real historical communities. In their own
eyes oikophobes are defenders of enlightened universalism against local chauvinism. And they view with alarm
the rise of 'populist' politicians who claim to speak for
the people against the political class – an alarm abun-
dantly illustrated in the reaction to the Brexit vote. But

they are animated more by hostility to the actual than by love of the possible. Oikophobia seeks a fulcrum outside the inherited society, by which the foundations of that society may be overturned – hence the flirtation with Soviet communism among the intellectuals of Orwell's day, and the radical Islamism of second-generation Muslim immigrants today.

What is needed, not in Britain only but throughout the Western democracies, is a serious attempt to achieve the kind of extended patriotism that will include as many as possible of those who are tempted in this way by the path of non-belonging. This cannot be achieved through politics alone, since it concerns the first-person plural on which politics depends. It is a cultural, and not a political task, and those who try to achieve it by political means – such as Marine Le Pen in France and Geert Wilders in the Netherlands – risk alienating the very people whom they wish to recruit, the ones who feel most isolated in the home that should be theirs, and whose sentiments are more likely to express themselves in angry rejection than peaceful accommodation towards their neighbours.

Social affections cannot be imposed by politics; but they can be influenced through discussion and example, through works of art and popular culture, through a concerted effort on the part of the patriots to give a genial and humane voice to their worldview – one that will include their critics in the work of nation-building. There

is a process of compromise and conciliation that enables
the deeply attached and the wanderers to live together,
and it is this natural process that oikophobia disturbs.

Major artists who have begun life in a posture of repudiation frequently turn towards acceptance and reconciliation, not by way of renouncing their criticism but
by opening themselves to the things that they share with
ordinary people. It was in this spirit that Benjamin Britten
composed his church parables and the War Requiem,
works that point forward to a renewed togetherness in
the aftermath of war. Many composers of my generation have been inspired by Britten's example, to write
music that presents the idea of a continuous and inclusive community in a spirit of affirmation. I think here of
the symphonies and string quartets of David Matthews,
the orchestral works of John Maxwell Geddes and Sir
James MacMillan, Robin Walker's *Stone King*, and the
recent operas that link to the tales and dramas of English
literature – Harrison Birtwistle's *Gawain*, for example,
Ryan Wigglesworth's *The Winter's Tale*, Oliver Rudland's
Pincher Martin.

In painting, as in music, there has been a rash of
repudiating and desecrating art – but its very designation
as 'Young British Art' contains a covert overture to the
British people, an invitation to join in the work of destruction and maybe to unite again in the wake of it. There is
no doubt of the ephemeral nature of this anti-art, and

of the far more durable character of the heart-touching work that is now becoming visible as the glare of the Young British Artists (YBAs) declines: David Hockney's celebrations of the middle-class living room, the hymn to the English experience that is Tom Phillips's *A Humument*, the civic statuary of Scotland's Sandy Stoddart, and the impressive growth of portraiture through the Royal Society of Portrait Painters. A few novelists and poets adhere to a posture of repudiation, but the story told by our best writers today is one of acceptance, searching in the folds of modern life for the places where sympathy can thrive. Thus it is with the highly popular novels and stories of Nick Hornby, Mark Haddon and Ian McEwan, with the poetry of John Burnside, Don Paterson and Wendy Cope, and with the touching cartoon novel that revisits Orwell's working-class England: *Ethel and Ernest* by Raymond Briggs.

The affirmative aspect of high culture links directly to culture in its more popular forms. We should not overlook the importance of historical fiction, such as *Wolf Hall* and *Bring Up the Bodies*, the first two novels of Hilary Mantel's planned trilogy, or the TV series derived from them. To those repositories of doctored facts we should add the many series devoted to the British legacy, of which Simon Schama's reflection on British portraiture (*The Face of Britain*) provides such a striking instance. The most popular soaps remain those that dwell with

affection on the ways in which our country has been settled — *East Enders*, *Coronation Street*, *Downton Abbey*, *Dad's
Army*, *Steptoe and Son* — while few recent television dramas
have had a success to match the Sherlock Holmes stories updated by Steven Moffat and Mark Gatiss, in which
modern London is re-immersed in its Victorian mys-
tery. Everywhere in popular culture, from the detective
novels and spy thrillers to the set-piece musicals such as
Oliver! and *Billy Elliot*, we find an unassuming domesti-
city of outlook, a recognition that nothing really makes
sense except against a background normality in which we
are all at home. And the world of the musical also shows
how eclectic and cosmopolitan this feeling for the normal, and sympathy for those compelled to depart from
it, may be. From *The Sound of Music* to *Les Misérables*, and
from *West Side Story* to *Mamma Mia!*, we find the world
of the musical reaching out across the globe to show that
what we are here at home is also what other people are
in the place that is theirs.

Yet, in the universities and the channels of elite communication, oikophobia remains, and has been a force in
politics out of all proportion to its place in the ordinary
citizen's heart. It takes the form of a refusal to accept the
human reality without first exposing the alleged injustice
on which it rests. Institutions and relations confer benefits on those whom they include, but not on the remain-
der. This innocent fact is rewritten by the oikophobic

imagination as a proof of 'social exclusion'. The love that
binds my family is inclusive. You, who are not a family
member, are therefore excluded from it. Of course,
exclusion is not the purpose, but merely the unintended
by-product of a benefit that exists only if it is not conferred on everyone. But that is not how oikophobes see
the world. For the exclusion that is the by-product of a
privilege can be made to look like its primary purpose,
part of a strategy of domination whereby old hierarchies
sustain themselves, exploiting and trampling upon those
whom they deprive.

As a result an entire inheritance of customs and institutions can be put in question, by those determined to
denounce and repudiate it. Aspects of the home culture
are denounced as racist, sexist, xenophobic, homopho-
bic, Islamophobic, and the invention of the 'isms' and
'phobias' keeps pace with the beleaguered community's
attempts to defend itself. As I noted, the accusers rarely
make the comparisons on which their case must depend.
Compared with which modern society, for example,
is Britain to be considered 'sexist'? How do the accusations of Islamophobia stand up in comparison with
the treatment of infidels in countries with a majority
Muslim population? Is Britain, which has received wave
after wave of immigrants in recent years, and provided
schooling, healthcare and social inclusion to all of them,
noticeably more xenophobic than Saudi Arabia, which

turns its back on refugees from nearby Syria and forbids all forms of public worship other than Sunni Islam, or Japan, which lets in virtually nobody at all?

Especially damaging has been the blanket charge of 'racism', levelled at British society by those determined to disrupt its major institutions. So vague and ubiquitous has the charge become that it is now all but meaningless, save in its effects. For a police officer, a social worker, a teacher or any public official to be accused of racism is to face the end of a career. Once accused, the guilty verdict follows, as it did in the case of Ray Honeyford, the Bradford headmaster who went public with the facts about the Pakistani-born residents who made use of his school, and who refused to accept the education that he was bound by law to provide for their children.[4] To suggest, as Honeyford did, that school education must provide the knowledge required in order to become an integrated British citizen, and that religiously motivated *apartheid* had no place in the curriculum, was enough to spark off the 'racist!' charge. No matter that race had nothing to do with it. No matter that there is no alternative idea of education that is remotely compatible with the intention of the Pakistani immigrants to remain and

---

[4] The case began with an article sent by Ray Honeyford to the *Salisbury Review*, of which I was editor, in 1983. Publication of this article eventually ruined Honeyford's career, and nearly ruined mine. I give some of the story in the entry under Ray Honeyford's name in the *Dictionary of National Biography*.

if possible to flourish in this country. Simply to affirm a concept of Britishness, however mild and undemanding in its outlines, is to attract this charge, the charm of which in the minds of those who make it, is that it has no definition, can be flung at anyone, and will always stick, since there is no recognized defence against it. Thus it was with the report of a Scottish judge, Lord Justice MacPherson, accusing our entire police force of 'institutionalized racism' – a charge that, because it targets the institution and no individual member of it, can never be refuted by good behaviour, whoever displays it.

Our country has been torn apart by this kind of rhetoric, whose purpose and effect is to give voice to resentments, by removing the right to discuss them. Resentment becomes a sacred cause, as it was for the Nazis, the fascists and the communists. And anyone who speaks for compromise with the existing order is targeted as the enemy. Something similar has happened with all the other isms and phobias. The adoption of 'Islamophobia' is the latest attempt to silence those who champion our inheritance of freedom and law against its extremist opponents. And it is preventing discussion of the most important problem now confronting us – the problem of our Muslim minority, and the jihadists who grow in its midst. I return to this problem in the final chapter. For the moment, it is only necessary to recognize the trick – the invention of a word in order to ring-fence a favoured stance against discussion, and to silence the majority by ruining the reputation of anyone who speaks in its name.

One positive result of the Brexit referendum is that, after the first flurry of the 'racism and xenophobia' meme, a moment of truth dawned on the British people, and even briefly illuminated the BBC. It was for a while evident to educated people that these labels designed to silence and to stigmatize are empty expletives, substitutes for thought, at a time when thought is more than ever needed.[5] One or two people began to make comparative judgements, to conclude that Britain is, after all, when compared with other communities, not a racist society, even if there are racists scattered among us, some of whom put themselves on display in the course of the referendum. It is not a society intolerant of minority religions – not now, at least, and maybe not seriously since the passing of the Catholic Emancipation Act in 1829. It has not, in recent times, been seriously anti-Semitic, and the upsurge of anti-Semitic violence and abuse has been due largely to Muslim immigrants who have yet to adapt to the surrounding culture. All in all we have experienced a moment of awakening, when our situation as a multiracial society with a large

[5] I say it was clear to all intelligent people, but it seems that Julian Barnes, surely one of the most intelligent of our writers, reiterates the charges against the 'Brexiteers' in their unmoderated form. See *London Review of Books*, vol. 39, no. 8.

number of recent immigrants has been accepted as the starting point for a free and frank public discussion. In these circumstances there are no 'enemies within' other than those who want to prevent that discussion from happening: the jihadists, the neo-fascists and the censorious liberals who cry 'racism and xenophobia' whenever encountering a worldview other than their own.

It would be foolish, however, to underestimate the impact of oikophobia on our national culture, and indeed on Western civilization as a whole. Repudiation, like affirmation, is a form of membership – membership among the virtuous and the saved. The dogma of the oikophobes is that no minority, no petitioner, no person on the margins should be excluded, and every barrier should be pulled down for the sake of the one who beats on it. This attitude has been active in politics, since the political arena is the only one in which it can be pursued without cost – the cost always falling on someone else, the small community that has tried to defend itself from the global tidal wave, the pensioners who wished to spend their last days among people of their own kind, the workers in industries that lower the cost of labour by importing a new and cheaper workforce.

Every inclusion is also an exclusion: however big the group there will always be a test of membership and those who fail the test will be excluded. A policy of complete inclusion, which repudiates every group identity, is a policy that does not recognize membership, and is therefore a policy for no conceivable community. It is the extreme of laissez-faire, which refuses to see what happens when people cannot find the marks of community in the world around them – namely civil war. The people whom Goodhart describes as 'somewheres' are those who recognize in their deep feelings that inclusion is the necessary foundation of social membership, and that the refusal to exclude therefore means the death of the community.

Yet, in all the pressures created by migration our political elite, egged on by the oikophobes, has dismissed as 'racism and xenophobia' any reservation concerning the constant inflow of people without any proven record of loyalty or any obvious reason to acquire one. It was the oikophobia of the university-educated elite around Tony Blair that led him to open our labour market to Eastern Europeans seven years before the EU required him to do so. And this attitude still plays a large part in the politics of Blair's successors in the Labour Party. In the wake of the Brexit vote, there is an opportunity at last to insist on the ground rule of politics, which is that inclusion means exclusion, even if inclusion is what it is all about.

This is not to deny that there are grievances, some of them long-standing, that we need to address. Nor is it to suffer the illusion that the overt and incipient conflicts in our society can yield at once to negotiation and compromise. However, it is at this point that we should revisit Orwell's observation concerning the British people, that they are more or less without religious belief, while retaining a core of deep Christian feeling. This, for Orwell, was the source of their observed gentleness and their 'eccentric habit', as he put it, 'of not killing each other'.

That observation is, in my view, of the first importance. For what the British have retained of their Christian inheritance is precisely that which is most needed in their post-religious predicament. The Christian religion is founded on a story – the Gospel story – and a religious ritual in which that story is repeated and sanctified, in words and music that imprint it on the soul of the worshipper. The story tells of a supreme sacrifice, in which the holiest of people gave himself for the redemption of sinners. It is not a story that incites violence, anger or revenge, but a story of suffering, compassion and self-sacrifice. The message of the saviour is contained in the words of the prayer that he taught us: 'forgive us our trespasses, as we forgive them that trespass against us'. The emphasis throughout is on this one idea, that we need forgiveness and will obtain it, but only through confessing our faults and forgiving those who have injured us.

The religious ritual is similar. Morning Prayer begins with a general confession, and is one long reminder of our unworthiness, offering absolution in exchange for the humble recognition that we do not deserve it. Over the centuries this unassuming ritual has penetrated the souls of those who perform it, so that confessing to fault and seeking forgiveness are the instinctive and immediate responses in every dispute. Our common-law procedures in contract and tort reflect this, with an elaborate concept of liability arising from reflection on the first question that arises for us in every disagreement: 'Who is to blame?' If the fault is ours, then we blame ourselves and try both to improve our conduct and to make amends. And in the little things too we prepare for confession, as in our immediate response of 'sorry' when someone bumps into us in the street.

I do not suggest that every British citizen behaves always in this impeccable manner. What I mean is that there is a model of good behaviour that we recognize, and which guides us in our dealings with the world. And it is one reason why the attacks of the oikophobes have gained such mileage. It is precisely because we stand at the ready to take charge of our failings that radical attacks of this kind make sense. Even if it is unjust to accuse the British people of racism and xenophobia, the accusation has a point: for being British they will listen to it, they will examine their consciences, and confess to whatever faults they come to recognize. Try throwing this accusation at the Islamists of Iraq and Syria: the only result will be a list of *your* sins, never a confession or a resolve to make amends. Indeed, as Czesław Miłosz writes in 'At a Certain Age', a telling poem about the destruction of the soul under communism, it is precisely the habit of confessing to our faults that is the first casualty of those totalitarian movements that warred against the spirit of compromise during the twentieth century, Islamism being merely the latest successor to them. We in Britain have successfully defended our free and democratic government, and with it our custom of honest self-criticism through public opinion, politics and the law. It is time to acknowledge this, and to take pride in precisely the thing that makes it so easy to accuse us, which is our habit of taking criticism to heart.

The readiness to account for our faults can be observed even in the worst of the imperial atrocities. Following the massacre at Amritsar in April 1919, a commission was established under Lord Hunter that was unanimous in condemning the action, as a result of which the House of Commons forced Colonel Dyer, the officer responsible, to retire – not a devastating punishment, certainly, but a punishment nevertheless, and one that accompanied a report that radically condemned the attitude and role of the British Army in India. The recent case of Marine Alexander Blackman, who shot and killed an injured Taliban fighter in the stressful circumstances of battle, is equally significant. Blackman was tried for murder and found guilty. Subsequently, as the result of a campaign by his wife, the verdict was reduced to manslaughter. Ask yourself whether such a trial would be even conceivable conducted by the Taliban (or by any similar entity fighting now) and you will know the extent to which justice and accountability have been impressed on our national character.

The weapons of the oikophobes are not confined to the isms and phobias, however. There is another and more subtle accusation that underlies their hostility to the existing settlement, which is the accusation of 'nostalgia', used as a blanket dismissal of any attachment that involves a heightened sense of the past. This charge has been levelled against all those who voted for Brexit – as much against the working-class communities in the old industrial towns of the North as against the alleged 'little Englanders' of the Home Counties and the advocates of the worldwide 'Anglosphere'. By nostalgia is meant the desire to return to an idealized world that was never as consoling as its remembered image, and which is in any case no longer accessible. The accusation of nostalgia is a ready, and often unthinking, response to those who hesitate to turn their backs on what they love, and it is worth pausing to ask what it really means and whether the thing of which it accuses us is really such a failing.

The word (from Greek *nostos* – the journey home) denotes the pain that people feel, when severed from the place and the form of life to which they belong. The capacity to feel this pain was regarded by the ancient Greeks as part of a virtuous character, proof of the loyalty that binds the individual to the community. The founding work of our literature – Homer's *Odyssey* – tells the story of a man who gives up immortality and life with a goddess to travel across dangerous seas to his *oikos*, to the home where his wife Penelope, son Telemachus and their household await him, so as to rescue them from the intruders who have tried to dispossess him. Odysseus turns from the immortal, changeless nowhere of Calypso's isle to the mortal, changeable somewhere that is his, to the place bound to him by the firmest of existential ties. To dismiss his longing as utopian is to fail to see that it is part of the most manly and courageous attitude to the future, in which the past is called upon not as a refuge but as an inspiration and an object of trust.

Our poets tell us that we arrive home 'so as to know the place for the first time', as Eliot puts it in *Four Quartets*, his great poem of homecoming. Turning for home is not an escape from the world but an affirmation of it – such is the theme of Hölderlin's *Heimkehr*, describing the return journey, which is also the forward journey into the place of belonging. In a thousand ways art and religion offer us homecoming as the true redemption. Those who dismiss this sentiment as 'mere nostalgia', and therefore retrograde, dismiss what we are. If there is utopianism and sentimentality in this confrontation it is not with the advocates of home and belonging but with those who imagine that human beings can live in a detached and universal nowhere and still retain the sympathies that make life worthwhile. There is a utopia of somewhere; but there is also a utopia of nowhere, which is the home of frozen hearts.

Still, the warnings against nostalgia have a point. It is right and dutiful to maintain the memory of home, and right to seek the way to rediscover it. But to live for a home that has been irretrievably lost is to live without hope or solace. And that is not to live at all. We need to take note of all the ways in which the world has changed, and in particular to avoid imposing on young people a vision of their country that corresponds to nothing in their experience, and which is rooted in a world that global forces have swept away. It is right to praise the virtues of a vanished world, as Stefan Zweig does so beautifully in *Die Welt von Gestern*. But it is wrong to advocate that world as a real-life possibility.

That brings me to the 'declinists'. A whole school of writing has emerged in post-war Britain devoted to telling the story of our national decline, a school typified by Correlli Barnett who, in a series of brilliant books, has made the case against the British elite and its education, telling us that the ethos, curriculum and lifestyle of the public schools and the collegiate universities did little or nothing to prepare us for the great conflicts of our time.[6]

---

[6] Correlli Barnett, *The Collapse of British Power*, London, 1972; *The Audit of War*, London, 1986; and *The Lost Victory: British Dreams, British Realities, 1945–50*, London, 1995.

The ideal of the gentleman, with its emphasis on fair play and honesty, left us at a disadvantage in the struggle against calculating and cynical forces. The classical curriculum put the modern world at too remote a distance from the scholar who had absorbed it; the downgrading of science and technology meant that we were beset by a crippling nostalgia, which caused us to gothicize our industry and surround it with feudal prohibitions. The education instilled by the public schools and the old universities has been, in Barnett's words, not a preparation for the world but an inoculation against it.[7]

In response, it is worth pointing out that knowledge advances largely because it is pursued for its own sake, so that those who make discoveries frequently have no use for them. But knowledge born as a luxury soon becomes a necessity, as the world adapts to receive it. Those romantic students destined for government offices in London did not at first know that the dead languages and ancient literatures which were the sum of their learning would be precisely what they needed in governing a world-wide empire. But Homer and Virgil endowed them with an instinctive sympathy for pagan cultures, and their knowledge of ancient history prepared them for their encounter with the African tribe. Out of their experience of applied ancient history arose the new science of

[7] ibid., *The Collapse of British Power*, p. 37.

anthropology. And later it was British amateurs, experimenting with seemingly useless things, who came up with the discoveries that tipped the balance of war: radar, the jet engine, and the first computer programs.

To return to my remarks at the beginning of this chapter, Barnett's complaints contain no comparative judgement. Set beside which elite did our elite fail so badly? In which country of the modern world do we find the educational system that compares so favourably with that provided by our universities? Which European nations, unhampered by the code of the gentleman, have shown us the way to successful empire-building, and retreated with credit from their colonies? All such comparisons point to the success of the British. By devoting their formative years to useless things, they made themselves supremely useful. And by internalizing the code of honour they did not, as Barnett supposes, make themselves defenceless in a world of chicanery and crime, but endowed themselves with the only real defence that human life can offer – the instinctive trust between strangers, which enables them in whatever dangerous circumstances to act together as a team.

Barnett's cavils fill only one shelf in the growing library of declinist literature. From Anthony Sampson's attacks on the old-boy network to Paul Mason's dismissal of the financial system, from Tom Nairn's warnings of the break-up of Britain to the description by David

Coates and others of our industrial decline, the message is again and again rubbed in that the British are falling behind, losing out, failing to be where they should be in the ongoing march of the modern nations.[8] But where, exactly, should they be? And whom are they falling behind? The problems that beset us beset all successful nations in the world to which we belong; industrial decline is simply another name for the worldwide change from manufacturing to service industries. The sense of social fragmentation is to be observed all across the post-Christian world as we strive to keep families and communities alive without the faith that previously united them. The network of 'old boys' who control the Russian and Chinese economies makes the British executive class look like a bunch of innocent boy scouts. And so on. The fact is that the repeated narrative of our decline gives us nothing to go on, no facts, theories or goals that we can turn to our advantage in the world as it is. It is 'a tale told by an idiot, full of sound and fury, signifying nothing'.

I have surveyed some of the criticisms directed at the patriotic sentiments on which I shall be calling in what follows. As I have emphasized, these criticisms make sense in part because it is in the nature of British people to go out to meet them. Although criticisms come more

---

[8] Anthony Sampson, *Anatomy of Britain*, London, 1962; Paul Mason, *Postcapitalism: A Guide to Our Future*, London, 2016; Tom Nairn, *The Break-up of Britain*, London, 1977; David Coates, writings listed on his website, davidcoates.net.

from the left than from the right, my response to them is not in the name of party politics, nor is it, except in the loosest sense of the term, conservative. Not all leftists are oikophobes, and the most persuasive of them might well agree with the argument of their fellow radical Richard Rorty, in *Achieving our Country* (1997), in which he argues that 'national pride is to countries what self-respect is to individuals: a necessary condition for self-improvement.' Rorty acknowledges the capacity of his fellow Americans for shame, but argues that we all should be involved with our country in such a way that 'pride outweighs shame'. Such is true of every country that can be seen by its citizens as 'ours'.

This returns me, however, to Goodhart's distinction. Can the anywheres be included on the same terms as the somewheres, in a settlement that emphasizes place as the source of citizenship? And which, the reader will ask, are you: a somewhere or an anywhere? I address the first of those questions in Chapter Six below; to the second I answer that I am, in Goodhart's taxonomy, an anywhere person. I grew up in the suburbs and moved after university to London; the first home of my own making was in France, and I could easily settle there. I came to the place that is now mine only twenty-five years ago, after decades of restlessness. Reflecting on my country I wrote *England: An Elegy*, which appeared in 2000, and which conveys my sense of seeing things from outside, as a visitor who is partly detached. I describe my settling in rural Wiltshire in *News from Somewhere* (2004), which tells the story of the people and the place around my house. The account that I give is again marked at every point by the outsider's desire to belong to a settlement that will always, in the end, be partly closed to him. For a while I was able to uproot myself and my family, so as to set up house, with the same longing to be part of things, in rural Virginia. Since visiting what was then Czechoslovakia in 1979 I have been a Czech patriot, and in the novel *Notes from Underground* (2014) I describe the torn homeland and sacred places of the Czechs, through the eyes of two young people who are searching for those things in the catacombs, and imbibing wherever they can from the hidden pools of belonging. In *I Drink Therefore I Am* (2009) I return in imagination to my spiritual homeland of France, while my most complete attempt to vindicate the national against the religious identity of a modern community is *A Land Held Hostage* (1987), which defends the Lebanese settlement against the creedal internationalism of Hezbollah. I roam the world in search of home, and am never quite where my body is currently resting.

For that reason, however, I am acutely conscious of the fact that place, and the networks that grow in a place, are the heart of belonging. Anywhere people need roots as much as somewhere people; the difference is that they need to discover those roots for themselves: such is the lesson of Simone Weil's poignant examination of the modern soul in her posthumous essay *L'Enracinement*.[9] The discovery of roots, when it occurs, lends strength as much to our neighbours as to ourselves. For it leads to the principal benefit that a mobile person brings to a place of settlement, which is gratitude for having found it.

[9] Simone Weil, *L'Enracinement, prélude à une déclaration des devoirs envers l'être humain*, Paris, 1949; translated as *The Need for Roots.*

5

THE ROOTS OF BRITISH
FREEDOM

It is a cliché to say that we live in a free country. But
not all clichés are false, and this one, it seems to me,
touches on a truth that lies at the heart of our national
story. The freedom that we enjoy is an objective fact,
and what makes it so is that it is concealed within the
very procedures of our law and thereby protected from
capture. Although we have a 'Bill of Rights', adopted by
Parliament in 1689 as part of the settlement following
the prolonged seventeenth-century crisis, and although
we also have a Human Rights Act, passed in response to
the EU's insistence on an explicit adoption of its constitutional orthodoxies, individual rights have been effectively guaranteed in our country since medieval times.
Several factors have contributed to this result, the two
most important, in fact and in legend, being Magna Carta
of 1215, and the Common Law, which comes down to us
from Saxon times.

Magna Carta required the monarch to seal a contract with 'the community of the realm', which meant

'everyone in our kingdom'. The contract was to be enforced against the king by a council of twenty-five barons, with the whole community under oath to help the council when required. Although specific rights were granted to 'all free men', with women and serfs presumed excluded, the Charter conferred on every man and woman without distinction a right to justice, protection against arbitrary demands for money, goods and labour, and freedom from forced marriage. It is possible to exaggerate the importance of this document, presented in strained circumstances by exasperated barons to a petulant king. Indeed, it rose to its current mythical significance only in the nineteenth century, and in the wake of Macaulay's *History of England*: significantly, Shakespeare does not even mention it in his play *King John*. Nevertheless it is the nearest we have to a written constitution, and its origins, as a petition from below rather than (as with the French 'Declaration of the Rights of Man and of the Citizen' of 1789) an imposition from above, endow it with a symbolic significance that is without compare among the records of our government.

Many of our freedoms have been inherited from the Common Law, which protects rights not by explicitly stating them and so exposing them to amendment, but by burying them in the procedures of the court. The presumption of innocence, trial by jury, and the system of appeals ensure that those accused of crimes have the maximum protection from abuses. Criminal procedure is adversarial, with the accused brought before a judge while counsel for the prosecution and counsel for the defence argue the case on equal terms, and the jury of ordinary honest people decides the verdict. This contrasts radically with the inquisitorial procedure of traditional Roman-law (civilian) jurisdictions, in which a suspect is brought before an examining magistrate (the French *juge d'instruction*), who may detain him for several months while collecting evidence. The inquisition may lead to an accusation and therefore a trial; but it may not. Although the inquisitorial procedure is disappearing now from much of Europe, it remains in France, and is responsible both for the frequent detention without trial of innocent parties, and for the comparative ease with which the French judicial system can deal with suspected terrorists. (The downside of our freedom is that criminals too enjoy it.)

From the earliest times the Common Law has been an instrument in the hands of the ordinary citizen, where-with to combat oppression. I have already pointed to the writ of *Habeas Corpus*, which is one expression of this remarkable fact. Although explicitly granted by statute in 1679, the writ has existed since the Middle Ages, and been available to all subjects of the Crown, regardless of their status as freemen or serfs. It is likewise with the Statute of Forcible Entry of 1381, which replaces a long-standing common-law right, and enables all subjects of the Crown to close a door on those who seek to invade their space. Indeed the Common Law granted such tacit rights to serfs against their lords that serfdom had effectively disappeared from England by 1450, three hundred and fifty years before it was abolished in much of the continent.

In civil cases the Common Law has evolved through the doctrine of precedent, not by explicit statement of principles dictated from above, but by the discovery of the rights and duties of the parties, as determined from the facts of the case and the precedents that bear on them. This too has contributed to the liberty of the subject, in ensuring that each case is heard on its merits, and judgement is construed as a concerted effort to 'do justice' to the parties, rather than to bend them to the will of the state. It is noteworthy that, unlike continental and European courts, our higher courts issue all opinions from the judicial bench, including the dissenting opinions of judges who voted against the verdict, so emphasizing the idea of law as something to be discovered through argument, rather than imposed by decree.

The doctrine of the Sovereignty of Parliament is widely declared to be a root principle of the British Constitution. But while the authority of Parliament underpins the judgements of a common-law court, the judgements are not made by Parliament, but by judges. The judges may be applying statutes, but not always;

and their decisions can be valid even when there is no statute that says so. This feature of the Common Law is in tension with the procedures under which the United Kingdom, as a member of the European Union, has been governed. And it reflects what might reasonably be called a rival philosophy of government, in which popular sovereignty is emphasized at every stage of decision-making. The British idea of government has been founded on the conception that authority flows upwards, from the citizen, through the courts, to Parliament and the offices of the state, and not downwards from the sovereign to the citizen. Hence British people have the unshakeable belief that anyone who, in the hierarchy of decision-making, has power over others, is also accountable to those others for the way that power is exercised. Accountability is the constraint within which all legitimate government occurs. From medieval times it has been possible to call on the courts to judge that some power conferred on an office-holder has been used *ultra vires*, beyond legal authority, and in that way to annul its effect. And the resulting feeling for law, as a possession of the subject rather than an imposition of the sovereign, has played a decisive part in our history, long before the clashes with the European courts.

Thus when James VI of Scotland inherited the English Crown in 1603 he brought with him to Westminster a conception of law that was, at the time, antipathetic to English practice. Scots law is a Roman-law system, which then emphasized the sovereign power as the fount of legal order, and so sorted ill with English ideas of Parliamentary government. Since the Act of Union in 1707 Scots law has been brought largely into line with the common-law jurisdiction of the kingdom, but the rift between the Stuart monarchy and Parliament was arguably exacerbated by the clash between the top-down and bottom-up conceptions of legal order. And this clash is part of what we witness in the British attitude to European law, as in the notorious Factortame case, in which Parliament vainly tried to protect our fisheries from Spanish poachers, and the legitimate grievance of our fishermen found no legal remedy.[1]

In civil matters, indeed, the Common Law is conceived largely as a system of remedies. The subject who has been wronged comes to the court in search of redress. And the common-law principle is that the court attempts to put him in the position that he would have been in, had the wrong not occurred. Awards of damages proceed according to this principle, and the concept of liability has developed in tandem with it. The sovereign is, in effect, the servant of the court in such cases, being asked to enforce the judgement, but not to make it.

---

[1] Factortame was in fact four cases, the crucial one being *R v Secretary of State for Transport Ex p Factortame (No. 2)* [1991] HL.

The conception of civil law as arising from the case-by-case search for a remedy gives rise to two further remarkable characteristics of the Common Law. The first is that the rules of law are derived from particular judgements, not the other way round. When a case has been rightly decided, judges search for the *ratio decidendi*, the principle that underpins the judgement. This principle may not have been stated by the judge at first instance. It may be a matter of discovery in the Court of Appeal, and it may even remain uncertain as to what the *ratio decidendi* really was, even though it is agreed on all sides that the case was rightly decided – in other words, that the right remedy was discovered.

Sometimes Parliament steps in to provide a system of rules, as occurred with the Occupiers' Liability Act of 1957. But these rules will be, as in this case, largely an attempt to summarize and render consistent the results of a large number of decided cases. The judgements in these cases will be, philosophically speaking, the true authority for Parliament's ruling. Many of the cases might be taken from the records of common-law courts outside the kingdom, as in this example, in which decisions of the American and Australian courts had a powerful influence on the Act.

The second remarkable result of this bottom-up approach to law is the emergence of another legal system out of the concept of a remedy itself. Principles developed through the Common Law and the king's courts do not cover every kind of wrong that a subject might suffer, and there thus arose the custom, in the Middle Ages, of appealing directly to the sovereign. The petitions were heard by the Lord Chancellor in the Court of Chancery, and were adjudicated by applying principles (the maxims of equity) derived largely from philosophical and ecclesiastical reflections on the idea of justice. Thus arose the system of 'equity', which grants 'equitable remedies' when the existing law can do nothing to help.

Two of these remedies are of particular concern in the present context, since they illustrate the extraordinary way in which the people have been empowered by the English courts to solve their problems for themselves. The first is the remedy, or rather bundle of remedies, subsumed under the idea of a trust. F. W. Maitland assessed the matter correctly: 'If we were asked what is the greatest and most distinctive achievement performed by Englishmen in the field of jurisprudence I cannot think that we should have any better answer than this, namely the development from century to century of the trust idea.'[2] Through equity the English law has developed forms of property that define duties without conferring rights of ownership, such as the duties of a trustee under

[2] F. W. Maitland, *Selected Essays*, London, 1911, p. 129.

a will; it has developed ways of dividing property and of recognizing the many interests that are invested in a shared possession; it has been able to protect innocent parties from exploitation by those who have charge of them through the 'constructive trust', which returns to the victim the assets that have been taken from him or her. In a hundred ways it has been able to acknowledge and to enforce forms of joint ownership and collective action that arise spontaneously among sociable people. Indeed, it has amplified and protected the associative genius of the British people, and has been a major cause of the ease with which they combine in the 'little platoons' extolled by Edmund Burke.

Thanks to the law of trusts people living under the English law can combine without asking permission from the state, and protect the resulting fund for the purposes intended. They can act as 'unincorporated associations' in the pursuit of their own eccentricities, and cock a snook at whoever chooses to disapprove of them. They can confer powers to act, and property with which to do so, on all the associations of civil society that appeal to them, without ever consulting officialdom: a freedom that has no real equivalent in France or Germany, where whole areas of civil action are governed by statutes that confer power on administrative bodies, so that citizens can associate for a purpose only if first permitted by the state.

The other empowering remedy is that of injunction. A petitioner to the court of Chancery could ask the court to intervene in the case of a threatened hurt — a libel, for example, or harassment short of criminal harm — by granting an injunction. This does not merely warn the other party of the civil penalties: it makes the threatened action into a contempt of court, and therefore a crime. In other words it brings the full force of the criminal law to the aid of petitioners, who in effect now address the person who threatens them with the sovereign himself at their side.

The extraordinary power that those two remedies grant to the citizen is well illustrated by cases of environmental protection in England. I will briefly discuss one of these cases, since it shows the way in which equitable remedies can trump administrative measures. One of Parliament's first attempts to deal with the problem of environmental pollution was by passing the Public Health Act in 1875 and the Rivers Pollution Prevention Acts between 1876 and 1893. These acts gave local authorities power to take criminal proceedings against polluters. However, the principal polluters were local authorities, which discharged sewage into the rivers without concern for the effect on the people and the fish downstream from them. Hence few prosecutions were initiated and the fines imposed were derisory. Subsequent Acts did nothing to rectify the principal weakness in the legislation, which was that it treated the rivers themselves as commons, in which no individual had an actionable right and which were by default the property of the state and subject to edicts issued by the state. In the years following the Second World War, when Britain was experiencing a socialist economy, with large-scale nationalized industries, compulsory purchases and massive privileges extended to any body that could be described as 'public', the rivers suffered severe pollution, and many of the most beautiful of them died.[3]

However, there was another way of proceeding. It had been clear since the case of *Chasemere v. Richards* of 1859 that the Common Law recognizes a right of riparian owners to enjoy unpolluted water along their banks.[4] So defined, the quasi-property right gives these owners a cause of action in civil law against those who destroy the natural condition of the water flowing past their land. It was a barrister and an angler, John Eastwood, who saw the opportunity that this presented to rescue the rivers from the state. While the penalties created by the Acts against pollution were seldom so heavy as to stop the offences, and could be administered in any case only after the damage was done, a civil action could be used both to stop pollution entirely and to prevent it

[3] The case has been lucidly set out by Roger Bate, *Saving Our Streams: The Role of the Anglers' Conservation Association in Protecting English and Welsh Rivers*, London, 2001.
[4] [1859] 7 H.L. Cas. 349.

before it occurred. This is because the courts could grant an injunction, issued prior to the offence, leading to a severe charge of contempt of court against the one who disobeys it.

Eastwood encouraged anglers and angling clubs to buy land adjacent to the rivers so as to be entitled to actions in civil law against those who were destroying their sport. In 1948 he went on to form the Anglers' Cooperative Association, which was to become the Anglers' Conservation Association, designed to offer financial backing to those who were in a position to initiate legal proceedings.

This kind of civic initiative is facilitated by the law of trusts and the common law of associations, which enable clubs to appear as collective litigants in a court of law. Hence clubs need no act of incorporation and no kind of permission from the state. Within a few years anglers around the country had united in the protection of their sport, and the landmark 'Pride of Derby' case of 1952, in which three defendants – a private company, a nationalized industry and a local government – were compelled to cease from polluting the River Derwent, awoke both industry and the state to the need to change their behaviour.[5]

---

[5] *Pride of Derby and Derbyshire Angling Association and Earl of Harrington v. British Celanese Ltd.,* *the Derby Corporation and the British Electricity Authority,* [1952] 1 All ER 179.

Such cases illustrate two great advantages of our bot-tom-up legal system. It is a system that empowers the citizen, and which permits problems to be solved where they arise and in a manner appropriate. Administrative decisions imposed from above do not have that kind of flexibility and in any case have the inevitable effect of dis-empowering the citizens who are best placed to under-stand and resolve the problem for themselves. It is often argued in favour of the European Union that, because environmental problems do not respect borders, and are suffered by all of us regardless of their cause, they can be solved only by transnational directives and regulations of the kind developed by the European Commission. If anything this is the opposite of the truth. Environmental problems are every bit as specific and concrete as any other, and every bit as dependent on the active inter-est of human beings for their solution. The EU's dictated 'solution' to a problem that did not in fact exist – the possibility of diseased meat entering the human food chain – was the directive that destroyed all local abat-toirs in Britain, leading by an inevitable chain of events to the destruction of British livestock farming by foot-and-mouth disease in 2001, at a cost of £8 billion.[6] The small-scale human solution was replaced by the large-scale bureaucratic order, and the result was both

[6] I describe the case in *Green Philosophy*, London, 2012, pp. 110–11.

unpredictable and uncontrollable, since no one involved knew what they were doing and all the old channels of responsibility were blocked.

The features of common-law jurisdiction to which I have drawn attention display what Friedrich Hayek calls 'evolutionary rationality'.[7] Common-law principles are not deduced from universal edicts formulated abstractly, but emerge over time from solutions discovered case by case. Like prices in a market, common-law principles are the by-product of indefinitely many decisions by people who may have no knowledge of each other, but whose behaviour nevertheless affects the conditions under which all of them act. The law emerges from the myriad small decisions, and is sensitive to the concrete circumstances that produce them. In this it has an advantage that might be called 'epistemological': it offers practical wisdom in the place of *a priori* speculation.

But this brings me to another point of friction between common-law jurisdiction and the European legal order. It is an essential feature of evolutionary rationality that it *adapts*. Adaptation is the ruling principle of evolution in all its forms, and this is no less true of the law than it is of biology. As the circumstances change, so does the law change to meet them; or if it does not do so, then it enters into conflict with reality. Bottom-up law of our kind is

---

[7] F. A. Hayek, *Law, Legislation and Liberty*, 3 vols, London, 1964.

adaptive by its very nature. In the Anglers' Association case it met the problem of pollution directly, while the top-down edicts of Parliament simply left the problem as it was. The same has been true of tort law throughout the modern period, and the kind of summary of adaptations that can be read in the Occupiers' Liability Act of 1957 is vivid proof of this.

National Assemblies and Parliaments can also adapt to changing circumstances, and their law too, although less flexible and more removed from the initiatives of the citizen, can answer to new problems as they arise. And if governments fail in this, they can be replaced, and in all probability will be replaced at the next election. But the same is not true of treaties, which lie on the legislative process like a dead hand. And the more the signatories, the harder it is to change, however vital the need to do so. It is this that added zest to the Brexit vote which, while largely a protest against undemocratic forms of government, was also in part a protest against the provisions in the treaties that have radically changed the aspect of many of our towns and cities – the clauses permitting freedom of movement of all people within the European Union.

I commented in Chapter Two on the effect of the 'freedom of movement' provisions, as creatively interpreted by the European Court of Justice following the Maastricht Treaty. These provisions have inevitably resulted in British people in working-class communities competing with foreigners for housing, jobs and healthcare, and sending their children to schools where English is the second language. The important fact is not whether they are right or wrong to resent this, but whether – if they do resent it – the law can take account of what they feel. The treaties cannot be changed, and the Common Law can provide no remedy against them. To people who have lived by the principle that the law is your friend, which brings the sovereign to your side in any conflict, the idea of an unchangeable edict dictated from some point beyond the borders of the kingdom is deeply unacceptable. Ordinary British citizens may not have the philosophy that justifies their feeling this way. But feel it they do. And their feeling it is a result of their legal inheritance, which has made law into an asset of the people rather than a means for controlling them.

Popular sovereignty is acknowledged not only in the procedures followed by our courts, but also in an unspoken assumption of civil life, which is that everything is permitted unless explicitly forbidden. This principle has been a driving force behind reform of the criminal law throughout modern times. The thought was made explicit by John Stuart Mill in *On Liberty*, that it is no business of the law to intrude on individual freedom, unless and until there is some proof of harm suffered by others. It is not for the law to prevent us from acting immorally or selfishly. Morality, not law, has the task of rectifying our conduct, and law can intervene only if that conduct threatens others.

You might think it obvious that the law should be bound by the principle that all is permitted, unless forbidden. But in a hundred ways legal systems depart from this principle, and when a system does so there are not always available to the citizens the instruments that would enable them to correct it. The criminal law of the communist states enabled the arrest and punishment of anyone, depending on whether the party and its agents desired this. The documented cases affirm that the principle underpinning the law was that everything is forbidden unless explicitly permitted.[8] Of course things are not like that in the European democracies today. Nevertheless in many of them it may not be clear in advance whether associations, demonstrations or educational activities are permitted, until tried in court. Home schooling, for example, is forbidden in Germany and associations must, in many areas, apply for registration and incorporation before they can recruit their members. In Germany you can move house only if you register with the police in your new place of residence,

---

[8] See R. Scruton, 'Totalitarianism and the Rule of Law', in Ellen Frankel Paul, ed., *Totalitarianism at the Crossroads,* London and New Brunswick, 1990.

and every citizen must carry an identity card and produce it on request.

The philosopher Leszek Kołakowski once half humorously summarized the differences among legal cultures as follows: in England everything is permitted unless it is forbidden; in Germany everything is forbidden unless it is permitted; in France everything is permitted, even if it is forbidden; and in Russia everything is forbidden, even if it is permitted.[9] The differences here are real, and part of what has made membership of the European Union so difficult for us. Precisely because law is the property of the citizen and not of the state, we interpret law strictly and apply it to the letter. Freedom of movement, therefore, really means freedom of movement. In France, Belgium and Germany freedom of movement is nominally permitted under the treaties; but everything is done to avoid the law, by imposing conditions on employment and residence designed to protect the local labour market from incoming competition.

This last point touches on a vital distinction, between states that do and those that don't issue identity cards to their citizens. In most member states of the European Union identity cards are required as a proof of residence, and residence is not granted automatically but often after searching enquiries into income and employment.

[9] Oral communication.

Undoubtedly the identity card has been an effective barrier in Germany, France and Belgium to the East Europeans who have wished to settle there, and also helped in efforts to pre-empt the plots of terrorists. However, when the suggestion is made that identity cards should be introduced into our country the protests always outweigh the favourable arguments, as the many voices insist that this will be the first step towards the all-controlling state. For the British every identity card bears, alongside the bearer's bio-pic, the face of Big Brother.

The suspicion of identity cards reflects a deep characteristic of British society, which is the connection between freedom and trust. Precisely because we are free to associate as we will, to build networks and institutions and little platoons without official permission or official knowledge, there is a premium, in our society, on honesty. British society has emerged over the centuries as a self-policing web of trust between strangers. It is because each member is free to bestow trust and to earn it as he wishes that this kind of trust emerges and becomes a secure collective asset of the people who are linked by it. Mass immigration of communities who do not build trust in that way – who depend on family networks like the Sicilians or religious obedience like the Pakistanis – has jeopardized the old legacy of communal action, and reminded the

British people of the downside of freedom. The freedom that creates trust can also, in the wrong hands, destroy it.

That said, it is important to value the liberty that the British people enjoy, to associate for purposes of their own. We are free to organize against the schemes of government, to form unincorporated associations, such as clubs, teams and charitable ventures, to found schools and colleges outside the control of the state, and to engage in religious practices that depart in radical ways from those currently established. The principles touched on above, relating to equity, trust and injunction, apply across the whole sphere of social life, and are responsible for the ease and immediacy with which the British people come together in a crisis, to provide help to the victims of disaster and institutions and enterprises that provide for some perceived social need. The difference between Britain and continental Europe in this connection is testified by the proportion of GDP devoted to charitable activities in the various countries. According to the Charities Aid Foundation's *World Giving Index* of 2015, measuring charitable giving by individuals as a proportion of GDP, the United Kingdom ranks top among European countries and fourth in the world after the United States, New Zealand and Canada, all three, interestingly enough, common-law countries. Italy comes

ninth on the list, Germany twelfth and France seventeenth, with the former communist countries all but
invisible.[10]

Freedom of association is one aspect of social trust.
We associate freely because our habit of doing so has in
general posed no threat either to the state or to groups
within the state. It rarely enters the heads of politicians
to limit this freedom, and all attempts to do so are met
with resistance. The same goes for freedom of speech,
which, to people educated in post-war Britain, has been
a firm premise of the British way of life. As John Stuart
Mill expressed the point:

> The peculiar evil of silencing the expression of an
> opinion is, that it is robbing the human race; posterity
> as well as the existing generation; those who dissent
> from the opinion, still more than those who hold it. If
> the opinion is right, they are deprived of the oppor-
> tunity of exchanging error for truth: if wrong, they
> lose, what is almost as great a benefit, the clearer per-
> ception and livelier impression of truth, produced by
> its collision with error.[11]

[10] CAF World Giving Index 2015, cafonline.org. It is worth noting that, according to
government statistics, 70 per cent of our population give their time and resources
in voluntary activity, 75 per cent give to charity in any four-week period, a third of
people are engaged in the democratic process, and nearly 90 per cent think that they
live in a place where people of different backgrounds get on together. Cabinet Office
Community Life Survey 2015–16.

[11] J. S. Mill, *On Liberty*, London, 1859.

That famous statement is not the last word on the question, but it is the first word and was, during my youth, the received opinion of all educated people. The law, we believed, would protect the heretics, the dissidents and the doubters against any punishments devised to intimidate or silence them, for the very reason that truth and argument are sacred, and must be protected from those who seek to suppress them. Moreover, public opinion has been entirely on the side of the law, ready to shame those who assumed the right to silence their opponents, whatever the matter under discussion, and however extreme or absurd the views expressed.

If that is changing now it is not because the indigenous British people have acquired a sudden desire to silence their critics, but because new forces have made their presence known among us – radical Islam and identity politics being the most evident. Threats to free speech in our country do not stem from our national identity or our legal inheritance. On the contrary, they come from minority factions that cannot easily live with those things and which for that reason are at the root of some of the problems that we are now confronting. Free speech is a sign of a strong first-person plural, which enables people who disagree over fundamental things to live together in a condition of mutual toleration. The growth of rival identities – notably the identity pursued by Islamists, who recognize no particular nation as their home, and the negative identities that have their natural home in universities – has caused the first-person plural to fragment, such that it seems no longer so safe to go public with yesterday's orthodox opinions.

Identity politics is now a fact of life, and in the next chapter I will consider its wider implications. But it is worth noting that, though the threat to free speech is serious, the British people have shown a strong determination to resist it. Our first-person plural is centred on the belief that we are accountable to each other, as people who share a land and the liberties that are protected there. The remedy for conflict is not armed confrontation but free discussion of our differences. The adversarial procedure of the common-law courts is therefore the model that we instinctively follow, whenever conflict looms. To silence one side to a dispute, we believe, is to ensure that the dispute will worsen.

Whoever wields power in our society does not possess that power from some external source – so we believe. He possesses it because we ourselves have conferred it. And because we have conferred it he is accountable to us, and will be judged by the law, should he abuse his office. Power, in the British conception, is never simply power *over* others, but always power *conferred by* those others, and any departure from this rule is resented – perhaps not consciously, but with a firm sense of the impertinence of the one who is bossing us about. And when it is clear that we have not been consulted, about matters, from the inward migration of whole populations to the gratuitous abolition of our ancient weights and measures, that affect us deeply in our sense of who we are, we become outspoken in our resistance.

The case of weights and measures might seem like a trivial matter, and of course, in comparison with the massive interference of EU legislation in employment law and business practice under the rubric of 'health and safety', weights and measures are not so interesting. However, the imposition of the metric system led to a well-publicized campaign of civil disobedience, and the feelings then expressed graphically illustrate the distinction between a society in which order arises by an invisible hand from free transactions and one in which order is imposed from above by a rational plan. It is therefore fitting to quote what I wrote on this topic in *England: An Elegy*:

To the outside observer the English monetary system [i.e. the pre-metric system of 240 pence to the pound] lacked all logic. To the English themselves, however, it was of a piece with their weights and measures, which were constructed by division rather than addition, and which therefore presented strange angularities of arithmetic: eight pints to the gallon, fourteen pounds to the stone, eight stone to the hundredweight; twelve inches to the foot, three feet to the yard and 1,760 yards, amazingly, to the mile – not to speak of rods and perches, gills and tuns.

Weights and measures mediate our day-to-day transactions; hence they are imprinted with our sense of membership. They are symbols of the social order and distillations of our daily habits. The old English measures once had their equivalents on the continent. But, the French Revolutionaries believed, they were symbols of a hierarchical, backward-looking society, a society that paid more respect to custom and precedent than to progress and the future. They were muddled, improvised, and full of compromises, in just the way that human life is full of compromises when insufficiently controlled. What was needed, the Revolutionaries thought, was a system of measures expressive of the new social order, based on Reason. Since the decimal system is the basis of arithmetic, and since mathematics is the symbol of Reason and its cold imperatives, the decimal system must be imposed by force, in order to shake people free of their old attachments.

The distinction between the imperial and the metric systems corresponds to the distinction between the reasonable and the rational, between solutions achieved through custom and compromise and those imposed by a plan. Muddled though the imperial measures may appear to those obsessed by mathematics, they are – unlike the metric system – self-evidently the product of life. In the ordinary, cheerful and yielding transactions between people, measurement proceeds by dividing and multiplying, not by adding. The French revolutionaries believed that by changing weights and measures, calendars and festivals, street-names and landmarks, they could more effectively undermine the old and local attachments of the French people, so as to conscript them behind their international purpose. The survival of the old weights and measures in England testified to the underlying principle of English society, that society should be governed not from above but from within, by custom, tradition and compromise, and by a habit of reasonableness of which the single most important enemy is Reason. The English measures were designed for the promotion of comfortable deals and just shares, and not for the convenience of the state accountant. They were of a piece with those great inventions of English law – joint ownership (conceived as a 'trust for sale') and limited liability – inventions which instead of retarding enterprise, as those with rational minds imagine, put England a hundred years ahead of continental Europe in the search for industrial prosperity.

As I wrote, weights and measures are a trivial matter when set beside such fundamental differences between nations as the hours of work, the school curriculum, town planning, housing policy and the protection of the countryside. But the example illustrates the rival myths of Magna Carta and the Vanguard as they are woven into the social fabric. Our society has advanced in an easy-going and sometimes shambolic manner, emerging from particular agreements and individual choices. Order is the unintended by-product of compromises and court-room disputes. It conforms to no plan but only to the constraints implied in our fluctuating agreements, including our agreement to reject those who have plans for us. The idea of order instilled in the European treaties is of quite another kind. It is order imposed from above, and passed down to civil society by a system of inescapable regulations, administered by a bureaucracy that is accountable to no one beneath it, but only to those from whom it is recruited, who have never paid the price of their mistakes.

Reclaiming our national sovereignty means reclaiming the culture of accountability. And to think that this will jeopardize our economic performance, our trade relations or our ability to negotiate a place in the world is to fail to see what British freedom has really meant to us. It is precisely through the exercise of accountability that we go most easily forwards, in economic relations as much as in ties of friendship and good will. To re-establish the principle of accountability once again at

the centre of political life is to take the first step to overcoming the widespread sense of alienation from government, and to placing the people – both the rooted and
the mobile – where they need to be, at the centre of all
the decisions that affect them.

6

THE IMPACT OF GLOBALIZATION

The past is constantly remade in the image of the present. We read our present identity into our history, not in order to discover the truth, but in order to replace one myth with another. When, in the wake of the Franco-Prussian war of 1870–1, the French became disillusioned with their national story of revolutionary triumph and Napoleonic *gloire*, the image of Catholic France, whose defence depended on acts of religious sacrifice, was disinterred from beneath the rubble. The new icon of the nation was not the revolutionary vanguard of 1789 or the heroic conqueror of 1805 but the peasant girl who had given everything for her country, as guide and inspiration to its king. The story of Jeanne d'Arc entered the literature, the art and the prayers of the French people, leading to her canonization in the wake of the First World War, when the French were struggling once again to come to terms with their stupendous losses. La France reassumed her feminine gender: the 'mocking and tender little girl who belongs to no one', as the Catholic writer Georges Bernanos described her.

In due course the national story reverted to its secular pattern, but not before the high culture of the country had been turned upside down by the Catholic revival. One of the last manifestations of this revival, Poulenc's opera *Dialogues des Carmélites*, adapting a screenplay by Bernanos, was composed sixty-five years ago, and it could not be composed today. It was a sincere Catholic's attempt to 'take back' the French Revolution. And it stands as a beacon above the routine anti-bourgeois literature of the post-war era, relaying an image of France that defies everything in the now official history. It is a poignant illustration of the way in which a reinvented past may briefly shine a light in the present, before sinking beneath the flood of new emergencies and the fictions designed to soften them.

I have dwelt on the past of our country, and the icons that embellish the old idea of popular sovereignty that we largely share with the English-speaking diaspora. But what do these icons mean today, and how can they be adapted to the condition of global communication and borderless commerce in which young people are raised? We read that the young voted by two to one to remain in the European Union, even if a third of them did not bother to vote. Again, in the subsequent general election the young voted in unprecedented numbers, organizing through social media and university networks in support of the radical oikophobe,

Jeremy Corbyn.[1] How do we interpret these facts, and what lesson should we take for our policy now? If there is to be a positive story told on behalf of the course that our country has chosen, it must be told to the young and by the young, with some hope of engaging their sympathy. And it must begin from an understanding of the many things that have been subsumed under the concept of globalization.

In one sense Western civilization, and its European heartlands, have been 'globalized' at least since the Reformation, when the freebooting adventurers roamed the world in search of trade and treasure, bringing law, force and empire in their wake. Free trade, the export of legal order, colonization and the transportation of work-forces, whether as slaves or as 'guests' — all such vast initiatives have created interdependent clusters of nations and colonies, the parts of which cannot now be understood in isolation. Contemporary historians are more likely to follow the lead of Fernand Braudel, Philippe Ariès and the 'Annales' school, studying geographical and geopolitical regions rather than individual nation states, and accepting that the great crises which shaped

[1] An ICM poll on 29 May 2017 found that Labour had the support of 61 per cent of possible voters in the 18–24 age group, whereas the Conservatives' share was only 12 per cent. Further, in contrast to the 2015 general election the young made a big effort to vote, particularly if they were in full-time education. Electoral Commission data show that more than 2 million people applied to register to vote in the weeks following the announcement of a snap election.

modern Europe – the Reformation and its aftermath, the new forms of scientific enquiry, industrialization, the revolutions of 1789 and 1848, the two world wars, the Russian Revolution and the rise of totalitarian dictatorships – could no more be confined by national boundaries than can earthquakes.[2] And what we now mean by globalization is simply the effect over time of a cherished principle of European law – the principle of freedom of contract, meaning one person's freedom to do business with another, regardless of all the physical, moral and spiritual distance between them, together with the law's obligation to uphold the resulting agreement. Industrialization was a step in this direction, enabling rural workers to move to the towns and exchange their labour for a wage. Imperialism was a further step, enabling industries to outsource many of their inputs, and to market their goods to distant strangers. The modern multinational company, such as Benetton, which outsources everything and owns nothing save a brand, is simply the latest move in the same direction – towards an economy in which everything exchanges in response to demand, and where locality and attachment are discounted.

[2] Note, however, Braudel's unfinished tribute to his native country, *L'identité de la France*, Paris, 1988–90, which is as heartfelt in its commitment to the national idea as the *Mémoires de Guerre* of Charles de Gaulle.

The interconnectedness of people has increased exponentially since the end of the Second World War, and new factors underlie and accelerate the process. These factors are rapidly changing the appearance and the efficacy of the old forms of social integration. The nation state, which seemed to open so clear a path to democratic government in the nineteenth century, may have as remote a character to young people brought up in today's cultural milieu as the laws of dynastic succession. All the same, the question about what to put in its place has received no consensual answer. On one interpretation, the European Union was such an answer; but in every issue in which national sovereignty has been at risk the EU has slipped away into the realm of wishful thinking, and the nation states have stepped forward in its stead – something that we have seen at every juncture in the migration crisis, in France's response to the regulations that threaten her state monopolies, and in the distress inflicted on Italy and Greece by their adoption of the common currency.

The birth of the post-war international organizations – the UN, the WTO, the ILO, the WHO, the EU, the OECD, the IMF, and all the other members of the Acronymia, as they have been described[3] – has led to a new class of transnational bureaucrats, whose task

[3] By Ken Minogue.

of controlling global networks has led to an interest in creating them. The scope for their ambitions has been amplified by the loss of local control. Prior to the Second World War national borders were an effective barrier to immigration, and a means to subject trade and foreign investment to democratically chosen rules. Today borders are porous, and indeed regarded by the EU as obstacles to its higher project, which is to abolish them.

New factors have been added to those, with effects that we are only beginning to grasp. First has been the shift of economic life: from local to multinational supply lines and production chains, from goods to services, from owners to managers, from saving to borrowing, and with all this the expansion of financial services to a vast industry in cyberspace, whose currency is the possible, the probable and the counterfactual. Second has been the growth of the information network itself. In 2006 only one of the six most valuable companies on the Fortune 500 index was an information technology company; in 2016 only one was not such a company. Some writers – notably Paul Mason in his book *Postcapitalism* – see these factors as marking a fundamental shift from the old capitalist economy, based on competition in the marketplace, to a post-capitalist economy, based on the sharing of stuff that is free.[4] I don't accept that theory,

4 Paul Mason, *Postcapitalism: A Guide to Our Future*, London, 2015.

which is too close to the old Marxist caricature of capitalism as a form of hierarchical control, rather than what it really is, namely the by-product of private property and risk-taking in the marketplace. Nevertheless, there is truth in the view that the new finance-based economy, dealing equally in real and unreal estate, in present and future assets, in debt and possession, has detached economic life from the real places in which it was formerly rooted. The stuff that is produced and consumed, that surrounds me in the home, that can be given, treasured, and fixed to a place, is somehow more temporary and interchangeable than the possessions of our grandparents, even though far more abundant than theirs. It is as though stuff itself has become insubstantial, appearing in its true nature only on a screen, and only when downloaded from the nowhere where it really belongs.

Things in cyberspace elude our attempts to protect them, and seem to be exposed to sudden and anonymous destruction. The financial crash of 2007–8 sent shocks through the global economy from which we are only now recovering, but with no confidence that the global nature of the economy was not part of the problem. For it looked as though nothing real was destroyed: the catastrophe took place in a realm of debts and promises, bought and sold across vast distances between people who had never set eyes on the real things or real people mentioned in the title deeds. The cyber-storm swept great accumulations of digits from one balance sheet to another, leaving everyone standing where they were, some richer, most poorer.

Yet more important than those factors has been the revolution in information technology. Information has always been an economic force, and attempts to own it and to exclude others from using it are as old as society. The grant of royal patents was the Tudor style of taxation, and copyright laws have, since the invention of the printing press, made texts the property of the one who first composes them. But the attempt to hang on to your intellectual property can achieve at most only a short-term success. Words, ideas and inventions can be used again and again without depreciation; they can be copied *ad infinitum* and they will leak from every vessel designed to contain them, to become part of the intellectual capital of mankind. This is especially true of those inventions that facilitate communication, which are fully effective only if also public property. Such was printing in Gutenberg's time, and such is the Internet today, promoted by software inventors who recognize the value to their enterprise of joining the 'open source' pool.[5] The attempts to own the new technology are fleeting and unprofitable. But the attempts to make use of it in networks of shared information now dominate the culture.

[5] See, for example, the Wikipedia entry under Linux.

The world after Twitter and Facebook is not the same as the world before and, whatever else is meant by globalization, the social media must be counted as part of it.

One important effect of this is the emergence of what one might call the 'network psyche'. Young people today do not see the social world in terms of established hierarchies, secured by boundaries, with a defined domain over which higher authorities exert control. They belong to networks, rather than places; they do not defer to hierarchies but to the peers and 'friends' displayed in the endless *mise en abîme* that they hold in their hand; and they live in a world of constant information, which arrives on their screens from everywhere and nowhere, demanding nothing in response to it save a message of the same detached and screen-friendly character. Although real events happen in their world, they know of them largely through the ripples on social media. It is not only advertisers who take advantage of this; terrorists too know that their product will be instantly displayed on a million iPhones and must therefore be made as gripping as possible.

The network psyche does not easily relate to a place; thanks to satellite navigation, it may not know what a place really is. Networked people do not find their way by observing and memorizing their surroundings, but by following the directions on their screens. They may know of the place where they are only from digital messages coming from outer space, and therefore from nowhere. Their location is not a place, but a set of instructions for ignoring it. Social media also abolish distance: friends and family in far-off places are, in their cyber-version, always near at hand, and this is a comfort to people who are without a fixed place of their own. Indeed, the overcoming of distance reflects a general truth about the network psyche, namely that it relates to others not through place and the things that endure in a place, but through the moment, and the things that shine in the moment from the anywhere that causes them. Networks erode places, and erase the hierarchies that settle there. They replace space by time, and time by a succession of crowded instants in which nothing really happens since everything only happens on a screen.

The world of the network is one without hierarchies of control. All participants have an equal right to send messages and to receive them, and it is all but impossible to filter things out – certainly impossible to impose any moral or spiritual order on what is essentially noise. Young people wander through networks that are full of lust, violence, hatred and spite, and they can avoid those things only by their own choice, and never because someone else is choosing for them. The sexual predator and the terrorist have equal chances with the teacher and the saint, and there is no point outside the network from which a higher authority can gain the advantage. The web is an unpoliced nowhere, a kind of Hobbesian state of nature in cyberspace. But for that very reason it cannot compete with the trustworthy somewhere for which all people yearn. It is a release from place, but not a replacement. Of course, you are free to leave it at any time; but it is built from links created by addictions, and its victims are caught up in it as flies in a spider's web.

In addition to this change in the human psyche there has been a corresponding change in the regime under which business is now conducted. Networks connect people by disconnecting them from place. And they confer advantages on businesses located nowhere. No doubt Facebook has a head office, but it is not in its head office that it is located. Nor is it located in the screens of its many users; it resides in the network. Like the brain it consists of billions of switches that may be linked in billions of ways, and which are never linked in the same way from one moment to the next. It is a broker among possible worlds, and resides nowhere among them. Such a business cannot be easily pinned down, and the question where it is, for purposes of taxation, legal accountability, and obedience to sovereign laws and policies may be decidable, but only by convention and without calling upon any basic loyalty of the firm. The arrival of Bitcoin and blockchain may facilitate this mass escape from the grip of sovereign overlords, by making currency itself into a network of freely associating users, outside the control of any state.

More and more businesses are built on this model, offering goods and services through networks that ignore national boundaries, coming to earth here and there like Amazon and Ikea, but only temporarily and only where the tax regime is favourable. Of course, transnational businesses have always existed, and shipping and insurance cannot easily be confined in a single place. But the advantages provided by the Internet, and by the ease of escaping any sovereign jurisdiction that insists on local accountability, have given rise to a new kind of business, which owes obedience to no nation state. The existence of such businesses and the networks that they exploit has given the international organizations an opportunity to control and regulate that they have not failed to take. Who else, after all, can really control these amorphous monsters? Hence the new kinds of business create a presumption in favour of government by global bureaucracies, which can impose a uniform system of regulation on all players in the market. Just as the people join networks without hierarchies of control, so do they relinquish attempts to control the businesses that have no other home than networks.

The anonymity of the global economy goes hand in hand with a certain spectral quality – a sense that the agents behind every transaction are not creatures of flesh

and blood who live in communities but discarnate corporations, who take no real responsibility for producing
what they sell but who merely stick their brand on it,
so claiming a rent on producer and consumer alike. It is
difficult to articulate this complaint, though it has been
made, with varying degrees of sarcasm, by a century
of writers from Thorstein Veblen to Naomi Klein – the
argument advancing step by step in order to accommo-
date the latest move towards anonymity. This economy
is not dislocated, as the nineteenth-century socialists
imagined, but unlocated. Yet it is for this very reason that
it troubles us. Economic activity has become detached
from the building of communities. We do not know the
people who produce our goods; we do not know under
what conditions they work, what they believe in or
what they hope for. We do not know the people who
distribute those goods to us, except perhaps as celeb-
rity CEOs – people who seem miraculously to escape
all responsibility for their products, which are not their
products anyway, but goods moving around the world
under their own propulsion, on which they have man-
aged in passing to stamp a brand. Local stores and local
producers are successively bought up or driven out of
business by the anonymous chains. And when a community tries to defend itself against the intruding giant it
finds that all the cards are stacked against it, and that yet
another anonymous agent, the abstract 'consumer', has

already declared a preference for a shopping mall on the doorstep.

And there is another complaint that people make, or which they feel in their hearts even if they haven't the knowledge to make it, which is that the anonymous corporation, which invests all its capital in a brand, thereby escapes liability for the long-term costs of its products. To put the point more exactly, the anonymous corporation can effectively *externalize* its costs. The cost of producing soya beans in Brazil – the cost in terms of environmental damage, devastation of the landscape, aesthetic and biological pollution – is not witnessed by consumers in the United States nor controlled by US legislation (itself responsive to lobbying from consumers). It is a cost that can be, as it were, left in Brazil – and left to the future generations who will have to bear it. This is a simple example of a practice that is in fact ubiquitous. The real cost of producing packaged food on the supermarket shelf includes the enormous long-term cost of non-biodegradable packaging, which might constitute as much as 25 per cent by weight of the shopping bag. This cost is not borne by the supermarket or its suppliers. It is borne by all of us, and by our descendants over the next one thousand years or so. You don't have to travel far outside a city to know what this particular cost means, and you can read about it in any study of plastic pollution in the oceans. But it is a cost that has been externalized. The personal factors that might encourage a trader, in local conditions, to behave properly in this matter are absent. There is no reward for good behaviour, and the costs of bad behaviour can be effectively passed on. It is surely no longer possible to doubt that this is a blatant feature of the global market economy, and one that is seemingly intrinsic to it, namely that it presents indefinite and expanding opportunities to privatize profit, while socializing cost.

A similar result of globalization has been an accelerated movement of capital around the world, as firms seek to secure their assets against the jurisdictions that might have a claim on them. Many of these assets are invested in real estate, wherever real estate is secure and protected by law-abiding communities and law-enforcing governments. Our country is one such haven, and provides, to those Russian, Chinese, Saudi and Malaysian oligarchs who seek to own a slice of it, the kind of security that their own way of doing business and their own jurisdictions could never guarantee – the security of a settled and self-policing community, at home in the country that belongs to it. Except that, increasingly, the country belongs to foreigners. We cannot blame the European Union for this, but rather the lax attitude to land ownership that globalization encourages. Land becomes a commodity, another form in which money is briefly crystallized on its way from one bank account to another.

Indeed, in our case, it seems that hardly any restrictions remain on the foreign ownership of our assets, land and infrastructure included.[6]

Free trade, as traditionally conceived, meant the freedom to buy and sell goods and (with qualifications) services, free from tariffs. The freedoms to move capital and people are freedoms of quite another kind, which permit both the ownership of the land and its repopulation by incomers. To suppose that the freedom to move capital and people is as much a part of free trade as the free exchange of goods and services is to jeopardize the very idea of trade. A business that comes into a country, bringing its own workforce, buying the land on which it conducts its trade but exporting the profit, and then selling the land again in order to move elsewhere, has merely used the country's infrastructure for its own purposes, but not engaged with it in trade. It has taken a rent on its place of residence, but given nothing in exchange for it. That is why, until recently, all nations have seen mobility of capital and people as a threat to national sovereignty and the security of local workforces. Since 1980 the world has been pushed in another direction, and one with which people and markets (a few multinationals excepted) are far from happy.

[6] See Alex Brummer, *Britain for Sale: British Companies in Foreign Hands. The Hidden Threat to our Economy*, London, 2013.

Nothing has value for the global market if it cannot be exchanged – neither land nor people are sacrosanct, and 'real estate' enters the market only if it can also join the 'unreal estate' dancing in cyberspace. Half a century ago it was all but impossible for a citizen of one country to own land in another. Now multinational dealers in real estate shift their assets from place to place, often buying up a whole section of a city and allowing it to crumble, in the hope of building some faceless tower on the ruins. The investment of foreign capital in choice real estate, combined with the ongoing influx of migrants, have had an unprecedented effect on the availability of housing and therefore on property prices in our country, presenting the British people with a vivid impression that they are no longer living in a place that belongs to them, even though they themselves belong to nowhere else.

All in all, then, the expansion of global business seems to be releasing economic life from the moral and social constraints that are at the root of localized communities. For the networked young this may not seem like a problem, since all is fed to them in any case from nowhere. If they feel an urge to influence or control what is happening, it is through petitions on the web, and not through the slow, patient procedure of old-fashioned politics. They are now so connected that every conceivable issue can be put to the vote directly, and decided by a few million clicks on the iPhone.

However, this plebiscite culture accompanies no real attempt to create and maintain durable institutions, which will take responsibility for the people's choices and account for those choices as 'ours'. The true political sovereignty of a people is not to be conceived on the model of 'consumer sovereignty' in a market: it is not a way of aggregating indefinitely many choices, but a way of *making* choices, one by one.[7] In our tradition it consists in the appointment of representatives who will consider the real questions that concern us and which we trust them to pursue. It is built on trust and has the maintenance of trust as its ultimate goal. That kind of sovereignty is part of being a genuine 'we', a first-person plural of mutual commitment. And it is a real question whether young people see a place for it in a fully networked world. Of course, they can use their networks to influence parliamentary elections too, and undoubtedly this happened in the recent British general election, in which Jeremy Corbyn was able to capture the vote of the young, and to achieve the entirely unpredicted outcome of a hung Parliament. As with the original selection of Corbyn as leader of the Parliamentary Labour

---

[7] The distinction here goes to the heart of political theory. Markets aggregate choices by the 'invisible hand'; committees and parliaments aggregate choices by explicit decision. Economists who refer to the first of those mechanisms as 'consumer sovereignty' are using the term 'sovereignty' in another sense from those who refer to representative government as 'popular sovereignty'. See Duncan Black, *The Theory of Committees and Elections*, London, 1958.

Party, the main factor behind his successful campaign was the Internet, and the ability of his young supporters to combine outside the meetings and committees of the old party machine. To that extent the astonishing rise of Corbyn from rebellious outsider to triumphant leader is as much a sign of the emerging plebiscite culture as was the unforeseen election of Donald Trump. But it is also a sign that representative democracy, with its committees and compromises, is giving way to direct appeals to the people. Indeed there is no clearer sign of this than the Brexit vote itself.[8]

Networked people may view with indifference the fact that they live in no particular place, or a place that belongs to anonymous others at the far end of the world. They may happily renounce democratic control over the businesses on which they depend; they may prefer a fiction of democracy through the online plebiscite while remaining indifferent to the workings of representative government. But at some point they will be struck by the unreality of their predicament. We have many Facebook friends, they recognize; we tweet and twitter in all our free moments; we enjoy an unlimited supply of unfiltered information about everything that may elicit our glancing interest; we can start and sign petitions to the people 'up there' who control the global machine.

---

[8] See Douglas Carswell, *The End of Politics, and the Birth of iDemocracy*, London, 2016.

But is there anyone we can trust? Where in this is the *real* friend, where is home and protection? Where is our community of belonging, and where is the political process that is committed to protecting it?

Those questions have as much force in the network psyche as in the emotions of more rooted people. This is suggested by the crop of nostalgia that grows in cyberspace. The question 'Where is my home?'[9] inhabits the network. Everywhere you search you find bids for community, which form and fragment in rapid succession, achieving stability here and there, but always breaking asunder until the moment – which may or may not arrive – when the promised community becomes an actual place. The question has been planted in the hearts of disaffected Western Muslims by the messages beamed to them from outer space, inviting 'brotherhood' for Allah's sake. And after all the fragmentary responses it finds an answer at last in some spot of earth, where the brothers can come together in an act of sacrifice. Online communities are more and more like places, in which some of the consolations of neighbourhood and mutual trust are being forged in defiance of the 'displacing' tendency of the social media themselves. Reactions to terrorist attacks also increasingly take the form of a reaffirmation of settlement. Protests over the recent

---

[9] *Kde domov můj?* – the first line of the Czech national anthem.

murders in Westminster and Manchester — including those from British Muslims — were almost entirely phrased from that perspective, as a reaction to a threat on 'us' and the place that we share, with placards everywhere in Manchester emblazoned with the slogan 'I love Manchester'. As noted in Chapter Four, surveys confirm that for people on both sides of the Brexit vote, place, job and family are the three things that matter most in any question of identity.[10]

The network psyche therefore has an obverse side, which is the desire to belong. Leaving aside the search for commerce and titillation, looking beneath all the clouds of vindictiveness and spite, themselves signs of a frustrated longing for membership, we can see that Internet searches are also bids for community. We are not yet used to the web, and all that it offers by way of virtual adventures and experimental contacts. But young people, like their elders, are in need of attachment, and share the basic human desire to settle down with those they can trust. To offer them the unreconstructed idea of the nation state is not to do justice to their condition, and for the most part they will turn away from the gift. The network psyche enjoys a 'view from nowhere'. Its vision of belonging is also beamed from nowhere, and those who share that vision will come to earth only when

---

[10] Information from BMG research on behalf of the Commission for National Renewal.

they have found the place, custom and neighbourhood that inspire them to belong. Trust does not come easily along a network, though fake trust can be tweeted in a flash from one end of it to the other. Hence real virtue, which does not declare itself but simply does what duty requires, gives way to 'virtue signalling', whereby the networked person gains moral status without the cost of earning it.

All that is, I believe, covertly understood by the network psyche, and a wise policy would be to focus on reworking the idea of a country and our attachment to it, so as to capture what is missing from the global fetishes, namely trust, attachment and safety. And here some inspiration can be gained from the aspect of Marxism to which I have just alluded. Marx did not criticize capitalism merely as an economic system, doomed, as he thought, to enter a terminal crisis. All that part of his critique was, in my view, misguided. He also criticized capitalism as a source of illusions, and in particular of the mystifications that lead us to endow commodities with a life of their own, and to address our interests not to real human life but to the fetishes that replace it. And one observation to be made about the web networks, and the social media that exploit them, is this: that everything they offer as an object of desire is in a certain measure unreal, a fetish that exerts a kind of enchantment over the one from whom its life is borrowed. This is evident in the great plagues that the Internet has brought among us – pornography, the culture of sexual display, and scenes of torture, death, beheadings and the rest to rival the worst of the Roman games. In these practices the human being is depersonalized, commodified, removed from the sphere of personal relations, to become a thing. But this thing is not a *real* thing, only an image in cyberspace, removed by an infinite distance from any relationship with the observer, who relishes the goods for which this image stands proxy but who does not engage with them in reality.

The screen and its networks can therefore be seen as merely the latest point in a process of alienation, whereby people learn to 'put their lives outside of themselves', to make their lives into playthings over which they retain complete, though in some way deeply specious, control. (They control physically what controls them psychologically.) And this is why it is so tempting to look back to those old Hegelian and Marxist theories. For they were premised on the view that we become free only by an act of 'moving outwards' (*Entäusserung*), embodying our freedom in shared activities and mutually responsible relations. The German idealists distinguished a true from a false way of 'moving outwards' – one in which we gain our freedom, by giving it real and objective form in personal relations and communities of justice, and one

(*Entfremdung*) in which we lose it, by investing it in objects that estrange us from our inner life. Their theories show how the thing that we most should value in human life — self-realization in a condition of community — is separated by a thin dividing line from the thing that destroys us — self-alienation in a condition of bondage.

The risk to which we are put by networks can be partly allayed by encouraging people to take responsibility for their lives and to join in the 'little platoons' of neighbourliness. But a full remedy must be spiritual: a renewal of the 'I to Thou' relation that lies at the heart of any true and durable social order. This is felt by many of those who succumb to the network temptation, and in particular by young people who are in the grip of social media. The voice that calls to them from nowhere is the voice of addiction, and therefore of loneliness, since all addictions isolate the victim in a condition of self-centred need. There is, it seems to me, a necessity to offer to the young a form of *real* belonging, one that does not flee into outer space, but which stays rooted in a place, and bound to those who have made that place their own. The longing for this is not killed by globalization: on the contrary it is part of what globalization *is*. Those who have lost a home will always long for one; and it is only those who have lived in the cold reaches of nowhere who know what somewhere really means.

It is indeed encouraging that globalization is seen by many young people more as a thing to be controlled and mitigated than a thing to be adopted as a goal. They witness the destruction of their environment by agribusiness, the spoliation of their cities and skylines by inhuman architecture, the uglification of their streets by adverts and logos; and they witness the escape into anonymity of the corporations responsible. Global corporations thrive in cyberspace while devastating the places and communities that supply their goods, and the young are the first to rise up against this. The network psyche, in its hunger for a home, reacts angrily to these spectral powers that destroy the homes of others.

Moreover, it is young people especially who have been shocked by the volatility of the globalized economy and the ability of its denizens to escape all liability for their misuse of others' funds. The financial crash of 2007–8 was in part caused by high-risk, high-yield loans, traded in financial markets around the world. National governments faced the collapse of key industries that had been 'too big to fail', and of banks whose liabilities were spread across the world and subject to forces over which the governments themselves had no control. Panic rescues and forced nationalizations led to a transfer of money from the innocent taxpayer to the guilty CEOs, who continued to collect their bonuses, and to sit at the top of their empires built of fictions. I don't say there was another remedy available. But globalization showed, at the time, its other side, as a social and political disease – a removal of the world's financial assets from the only thing that can make people truly accountable for the use of them, namely the place where they can be located, and the law of the land on which they sit.

There is also a growing perception among the young that globalization means Americanization, which in turn means the surrender of the European inheritance to unrestrained market forces, regardless of the European people and with scant respect for their treasures.''Those who tell us, like Tony Blair in his speech to the Labour Party conference in 2005, that globalization is inevitable and that to resist it is to stand against the tide of history, forget that it is simply the latest phase of a continuous process that we must manage, and have in the past tried to manage for our collective benefit. When, during the early nineteenth century, industrialization began to accelerate, the response was not simply to acquiesce in everything, the destruction as much as the creation. On the contrary, people were moved to combine against the destruction – to campaign for laws restraining the employment of children and governing the hours of work, for laws protecting the landscape and

---

'' On the inherent confrontation between Americanization and European culture see the evocative study by George Steiner, *The Idea of Europe*, London, 2004.

the historic buildings of the cities, and so on. And the campaigns were based on *national* feelings – on the desire to protect communities and their settlements from the global market forces. Such is precisely what is implied in the name of the National Trust.

We should also recognize that the extent of economic globalization has been exaggerated. Less than 25 per cent of global economic activity is international, and foreign direct investment accounts for less than 10 per cent of all fixed income worldwide. Following the financial crisis, global connectedness has yet to return to pre-2007 levels.[12] And some argue that, with the spread of automation, the economy will become less rather than more global.[13] Whatever the truth about that, it seems to me that we have been massively misinformed by propaganda from the politicians and the lobbyists, who wish us to accept as inevitable something that is not inevitable at all, but merely one input into the compromise that will do justice to our many interests. Globalization results from relaxing controls that had been in place for centuries, and which would have remained in place had politicians not joined in the factitious excitement. To say that we must simply go along with it, to say, with Tony Blair, that 'the character of this changing world is

[12] See in general David Goodhart, *The Road to Somewhere: The Populist Revolt and the Future of Politics*, London, 2017, Chapter 4.
[13] See for example Finbarr Livesey, *From Global to Local*, London, 2017.

indifferent to tradition', is to betray the profession of politics. It would be as though Disraeli, Shaftesbury and Lord John Manners had joined forces with the factory owners in order to press for yet longer hours of work in the factories from yet younger children, on the grounds that all resistance to market forces is futile.

There is no more vivid symbol of globalization than the glass and steel architecture that has thrust itself into the streets and skylines of our cities, and it is precisely from this aspect of the phenomenon that we should be guided in our resistance to it. When Le Corbusier began his campaign on behalf of the 'international style' it was with a plan to destroy all Paris north of the Seine and replace the city with a network of concrete towers. The plan is inevitable, he told the city authorities, it speaks of necessities, and it must be adopted. The city authorities were not convinced, and Le Corbusier went away in a huff, brooding on a new plan to destroy Algiers instead.[14] We see in the city of Paris, constantly renewed, yet always the same, a centre of resistance to the global project. Paris is the perfect example of somewhere, a home to its residents and a lesson to the multinationals that they too should work from home. Unlike London, with its random scattering of magnified kitchen gadgets,

---

[14] See John R. Silber, *Architecture of the Absurd: How 'Genius' Disfigured a Practical Art*, London, 2007.

and its skyline like a mouth of broken teeth, Paris represents a precipitation of social capital in architectural form. This social capital, infinitely more valuable than the cyber capital of the global predators, will last just as long as the city's residents continue to defend it.

It is worth pointing out that most of the propaganda on behalf of globalization reflects a narrow vision of economic value. The social capital to which I have just referred is crystallized in the beauty, harmony and dignity of Paris. Those qualities bring people to live and work in the city, to visit it and spend in it, to exist within its periphery in a heightened and creative way of being. You could knock down parts of Paris and build faceless towers, bringing corporate investment and employment, and the value of this will no doubt be high in monetary terms. Moreover the loss would be said, at the time, to be of no financial significance – 'merely aesthetic', like the loss in the last few years of the city of London. But that is only because losses of this kind do not *have* financial significance. Their economic value infuses the entire life of the city, and lasts forever, being dependent on no particular business and no particular commercial networks.

The real economic value that comes from resisting global finance is in this case incalculably greater than the value that comes from giving way to it. And the case is again exactly parallel to the resistance in Victorian

Britain. Of course there was a huge financial sacrifice involved in limiting the hours of work in the factories to ten in a day, in providing education and medical care to the children involved, and in respecting holidays and family reunions. Those who campaigned for these things were enemies of the market. But they were the friends of economic value, for they worked to preserve and enhance the social capital contained in the family, in recreation, in learning and neighbourhood. Their success helped to create the settled and patriotic working class described by Orwell. And, as he rightly argued, the long-term stability and prosperity of the kingdom depended precisely on this incalculable asset.

If we are to mitigate the effects of globalization in its latest phase therefore – the phase in which people and their settlements are treated as exchangeable objects – the humane and patriotic resistance mounted in the nineteenth century must be mounted again. Young people may yet recognize this, and accept that the answer to globalization is neither the American free-for-all nor the top-down socialist plan, but a new set of side-constraints, like the planning laws that have saved the city of Paris. Such side-constraints are inherently local in character, exercises of sovereignty in the face of outside attempts to knock down the barriers. The solution is not to embrace globalization without reserve, but to set *limits* to it, and to fortify the walls that hold the limits in place.

Part of the appeal of the European Union is that it has aimed for a set of regulations that could be interpreted in that way, as containing the global process and where possible returning the costs of bad behaviour to those who incur them. But this observation points to the real problem buried in the folds of globalization – which is the tendency to reach for global rather than local ways of countering it. For many young people, especially in Britain and Germany, globalization is another name for 'neo-liberalism', itself the latest incarnation of international capitalism. And to resist capitalism, they suppose, we need a global system of control, so as to regulate the networks that pose the principal threat to those who have no say in the present scheme of things. The youth vote for Jeremy Corbyn was a vote against capitalism. It was emphatically not a vote for the nation, as the true counter to global networks. Likewise, the youth vote to remain in the European Union was a vote to control the capitalists, the financiers and those who had supposedly brought about the economic crisis of 2007–8. It was a vote for a global response to a global problem, and not for a rival centre of loyalty. It was premised on the assumption that business must be subject to constraints that operate across the traditional boundaries.

Things are somewhat different in France, where the reaction of the young against *mondialisation* has been if anything more radical than the reaction in Britain. Those on the left believe, like their British contemporaries, that we are confronting capitalism in its latest form, part of the neo-liberal demon born in America. Those on the right, however, see globalization as an assault on France and its cultural heritage, and it is significant that a large number of young people in France supported Marine Le Pen in the first round of the 2017 presidential elections, on the grounds that she spoke for France against its dilution by the global market. While those on the French left remain attached to Marxist nostrums, and therefore to internationalism in another version, those on the right are clear that globalization is first and foremost a threat to national identity. The combat, for the latter, is not that of the proletariat against the bourgeoisie, but that of France against the culture of nowhere.

The French attitude to globalization has also been ambivalent, and has undergone a radical overhaul in the last two years. The intellectuals of a previous generation were brought up on the leftist literature – from Guy Debord to Jean Baudrillard – that seems to welcome the commodification of the world with tongue in cheek.[15] The *Communist Manifesto*'s ironical celebration of capitalism, as the agent by which 'all that is solid melts into air', became an ambiguous welcome extended by Debord to

[15] See Guy Debord, *La société du spectacle*, Paris, 1967, Jean Baudrillard, *Simulacres et simulation*, Paris, 1981; G. Lipovetsky and J. Serroy, *L'esthétisation du monde*, Paris, 2006.

the society of the 'spectacle' and by Baudrillard to the culture of the 'simulacrum'. Jean Serroy and Gilles Lipetsky went further, offering a sarcastic celebration of the 'aestheticization of the world'. The principal objects of manufacture in today's consumer society, they tell us, are not objects of use, but appearances, representations, images, which hold our attention just long enough to claim our money, before being replaced by the next illusion. The global economy, they argue, deals largely in representations, as products are absorbed into their brand names, and worldwide images blot out the trade in mere things.

Such ironical commentaries do nothing either to present an alternative to globalization or to fortify young people against the worst effects of it. The hearts of the young are increasingly turned in another direction, and many are beginning to look for cultural figures and politicians who might help them to take a stand.[16] Modern France has a tradition of extra-Parliamentary protests, and indeed began with one. And these protests are invariably led by the young. The interesting thing is that, in recent times, the young have been demonstrating on behalf of national values against the cosmopolitan orthodoxy. The million-strong *manif pour tous*, on behalf of the traditional family and against gay marriage, was

[16] See the new journal *Limite*, for example, which advocates an integral ecology, in which the human settlement is defended alongside the natural environment.

organized and led by the young. It is young people who form the core of the *mouvement identitaire*, and it is young people who are most inspired by the small-scale travelling assemblies of '*veilleurs*', who gather in public places to read the literature of their country and to meditate on its spiritual heritage. The political effects of this are significant, as we have seen in the recent presidential elections, in which young people – whether voting for the radical Marxist Jean-Luc Mélenchon or for the nationalist Marine Le Pen – showed their rejection of the globalizing vision of their country promoted by the former political establishment.

As I indicated in Chapter One, identities are the imprint left by social membership. Some groups offer no more than joint activity, like cricket clubs. Others create loyalties of an existential kind – even a willingness to die for the group, as with many cults and religions. Some groups also make decisions on behalf of their members. This is true of clubs and teams, though not as a rule of religions; it is also and pre-eminently true of nations, which do not merely decide for the citizens but also coerce their obedience. The state, which is the nation in its political aspect, makes decisions in the name of its citizens, and is accountable to them in doing so. The citizens, who compose the nation in its social aspect, are obliged to obey the state, regardless of their opinion as to the rightness of its orders.

The great transformations that I have touched on in this chapter have had the effect of weakening national identities, but without producing any rival centre of command. And it is this fact above all that has contributed to the volatility of Western electorates. People are recruited to decisions that do not correspond to their other forms of membership. Some react to this with vociferous protests, crying 'not in my name', as in response to the election of Donald Trump, and to the Brexit vote. Others react with passive resentment, which simmers quietly until the chance comes to express itself – as again we witnessed, though on the other side, in the Brexit vote.

This weakening of national identities, which is to be observed all across the Western world, opens the path to 'identity politics'. Instead of acquiescing in a shared public culture and uncomplaining acceptance of the national idea, people begin to espouse rival identities that challenge the existing order of things, and to put those identities on display. Two examples illustrate what I have in mind: the Muslim identity assumed by many British second-generation immigrants, and the 'gay' identity expressed by many campaigners for gay rights. As has often been pointed out, Sunni Islam confers a strong, almost inviolable sense of membership; but it does not define a set of offices whose pronouncements are made in the name of the faithful. (The Shi'a alternative, as developed by the Ayatollahs of Iran, is nearer to the Christian

Church in this respect, though even the Shi'ites are without a legally recognized corporate person, in other words, a Church, that makes decisions in their name.) The quandary for many European Muslims is that their preferred identity issues in no political decisions, while the political decisions made in their name presume an identity that may have no real meaning for them.

Gay activists by contrast, while making much of their identity, do not really mind that there is no institution that makes decisions in their name – no gay parliament, for example. For their goal is to secure a niche within the nation state, where their interests can be represented in the general law-making process. But as minority identities of this kind proliferate, national identities lose some of their hold. The French *manif pour tous* was a response to this – an attempt by young people to affirm a traditional and national identity against a rival claim for political recognition.

The volatility of the democratic process today reflects those facts. And the rise of negative identities – identities shaped by a sense of exclusion – explains the decline of free speech on campus. The demand to be included becomes a vehement condemnation of the old excluder, and the desire to silence, to censor and even to threaten and punish comes from the pursuit of an identity that needs publicly to emphasize its oppositional stance. In the volatile moment through which we are living we must expect, therefore, a continual fragmentation of identities, combined with a growing censorship and even violence against those who define themselves in the old and national way.

At the same time, as I have emphasized throughout, we have no inclusive identity other than the one provided by national sentiment and the popular sovereignty that has been rooted in it. What is happening in France may therefore begin to happen elsewhere. The search for identity, and the valuing of identity against the demands of global commerce, is likely to become the critical factor in national elections. Indeed, realistically minded economists have begun to put identity into their equations, even into equations expressed as 'utility functions'.[17] And although identities compete and not all of them aim for sovereignty, national identities are beginning to emerge at the top of the political wish list. The European Union has taken much of the political process away from elected politicians, but the result has not been a surge of identification with the European institutions. On the contrary, those institutions have given a kind of regulative shelter to separatist parties in Catalonia, Scotland and Flanders, and to regionalist parties in Italy. Such parties promise a retreat from globalization and a

[17] See George A. Akerlof and Rachel E. Kranton, *Identity Economics: How Our Identities Shape Our Work, Wages and Well-being*, Princeton, 2010.

reaffirmation of the identities that linger just below the surface of political bargaining. What this will mean in the long run is anyone's guess. But it is surely a sign that globalization, even for the networked generation, is a force to be governed, not a command to be obeyed. All that I can conclude from that brief excursion into identity politics, therefore, is that we must do our best to unite behind a conception of what we share, rather than what divides us. How to do this is the topic of my final chapter.

7

OUT INTO THE WORLD

The argument is often made that Britain belongs in Europe and will be bereft of its true identity if it leaves the Union. This argument assumes precisely what is most questionable, namely that Europe is the same thing as the European Union. On the contrary, the EU is – from the point of view of European history and culture – an aberration, a falling away from the great achievement of European civilization in creating the sovereign nation state. In this endeavour Britain was perhaps first in the field, and our continental partners would have caught up with us in the nineteenth century had it not been for the Napoleonic conquests, the resulting rise of Prussia and the ensuing Franco-German enmity. The adoption of a transnational government, based on centralized decisions imposed through a top-down system of regulations, was understood as a response to that enmity which, by 1945, had run its course. But this metrication of our social and political inheritance is precisely what is least European in the regime from which we are releasing ourselves.

Europe is not just a geographical region – it is not even a geographical region. It is a civilization, which grew from Roman imperial government and the Christian Church, and which took on its distinctively modern form in the wake of the Enlightenment, when the idea of the citizen first emerged from behind that of the nation state. As I mentioned in Chapter Two, in law the British are not citizens of their country, but subjects of the Queen. The term 'citizen', used by the French revolutionaries, was a deliberate rebuke to monarchical authority. But I have been using the term in a wider sense, to denote a feature of European political order exemplified as much by constitutional monarchies as by the republics that have largely replaced them, namely the mutual accountability of the individual and the government.

Citizens live in two spheres: the private and the public. To the first sphere belong the choices and values that shape their individual destinies, to the second belong the laws and institutions that permit the peaceful coexistence of the many forms of private life. Religion belongs in the first of those spheres: it may be, and perhaps ought to be, acknowledged in the public realm, but is not now the source of public order, even though all our public institutions bear the stamp of the Christian inheritance.

This separation of spheres was laid down by Christ himself, in the parable of the Tribute Money ('Render unto Caesar what is Caesar's, and to God what is God's'), was taken up by the early Church, with the 'two swords' doctrine of Pope Gelasius I, and acknowledged in the long conflicts between Pope and Emperor, Church and State, which ended with the final triumph of secular government at the Enlightenment. This history is internal to the European experience: it tells us that individuals are morally autonomous and publicly responsible, free to realize their conception of the good in private, but obedient in public to laws that aim to guarantee the freedom of all.

Equally important is the Judaeo-Christian morality, summarized in Leviticus: 'Thou shalt love the Lord thy God with all thy heart and with all thy soul and with all thy mind and with all thy strength, and thou shalt love thy neighbour as thyself.' On these two commandments, Christ added, hang all the law and the prophets. Translated into modern idiom the commandments correspond to the two spheres of human life. In the first sphere – the sphere of what we are for ourselves – we are consecrated to the highest good. In the second – the sphere of what we are for others – we are bound by the principle of neighbour love.

The idea of neighbour love was reformulated at the Enlightenment by Kant as the categorical imperative: act only on that maxim which you can will as a law for all rational beings, and treat humanity, whether in yourself or in another, never as a means only but always as an end in itself. These principles are brought together in the prayer on which Europeans from time immemorial have been raised, which asks God 'to forgive us our trespasses as we forgive them that trespass against us'.

It is surely plausible to suggest that the two commandments and the Lord's Prayer form the moral, spiritual and emotional foundation of the thing that comes naturally to Europeans, namely recognition of the Other as other than you. We are commanded to love our enemy, to pursue forgiveness and to accept the rule of secular powers. Those precepts lead of their own accord to equality before the law, to religious toleration and to popular sovereignty. But they also embody a distinctive vision of human beings, as free and accountable individuals, answerable for their faults, but duty-bound to respect the freedom and otherness of their neighbours. They form the precious core of our social capital, and it would be a tragic day for Europe should that capital be squandered or repressed by the regulative machine that has been set up to invest it.

The European heritage is often confounded with 'liberal individualism': the view of human society as composed of free individuals, gathered together by a social contract, for whom there are no inherited barriers or obligations, and who recognize no source of validity in any human arrangement beyond the free choice of its participants. That view has a convenient and quasi-mathematical purity. But, as Hegel showed, it ignores the situated character of human freedom.[1] We are not born free, nor do we come into this world with a self-identity and autonomy of our own. We *achieve* those things, through the conflict and cooperation that weave us into the social fabric. We become freely choosing individuals only by acquiring obligations to parents, siblings, institutions and groups: obligations that we did not choose. The Enlightenment should not be seen as a repudiation of inherited identities, but as a way of affirming them. For they are integral to the only kind of freedom that really matters — the freedom of responsible individuals, accountable to their kind. It is through the encounter with others that true self-knowledge and self-identity are acquired, and institutions, laws and religion all play their part in shaping the freedom of the truly autonomous individual. Political freedom, in the European sense, is *situated* freedom, freedom marked by the customs and institutions that have emerged from free association over centuries.

That idea is not specifically Christian, though it owes much to the Christian idea of neighbour love. It has Jewish as well as Christian roots, and it is not far-fetched

---

[1] I refer here to the argument of Hegel's *Phenomenology of Spirit*, and *Philosophy of Right*. The philosophy of the Other has pursued a winding and fascinating course in recent times, and has been especially influential in France, thanks to Alexandre Kojève, and to those who attended his interwar lectures: Levinas, Lacan, Sartre and de Beauvoir especially.

to find a comparable notion in the writings of Kant's friend and correspondent Rabbi Moses Mendelssohn, who was in turn the inspiration for Gotthold Lessing's humane defence of secular law and religious toleration, *Nathan the Wise* (1779). Mendelssohn's public-spirited grandson Felix was a treasured representative of our Enlightenment culture, who took up the educational mission of Goethe and Schiller, rescued Bach for posterity, absorbed our religious traditions, Christian and Jewish, and incorporated them, through the Gewandhaus and the Musikhochschule in Leipzig, into the public art of choral music. Felix belonged to a great movement of ideas and feelings, stretching from the Hebrides to the Mediterranean, the effect of which was to translate our spiritual heritage into the literary, musical and artistic idioms that form the core of our romantic legacy. We, who are heirs to the labour of people such as Goethe, Mendelssohn, Wordsworth, Scott, Chateaubriand, Manzoni and Mickiewicz, often fail to appreciate their achievement, which was to transform religion into culture, and the hope of eternity into a vision of coexistence in the here and now.

That vision was not devoted to the idea of abstract and universal humanity, divorced from all specific obligations and traditions, despite what is often said about the Enlightenment. It was rooted in the sense of place, and shared citizenship. It has been incorporated into the legal

systems of Europe, both the continental Roman-law traditions and the common-law and custom-based idioms
of England and Scandinavia. Both systems are territorial,
and they borrow the Roman-law concept of the person
to describe individual human beings as accountable for
their lives and actions. The same vision of the responsible
individual has inspired European art and literature since
the Renaissance, and it underlies the distinctive achievements of European civilization in the fields of science and
politics. But the focus of the vision is not *Europe* at all. Its
focus is twofold: on the one hand the free individual,
sovereign over his or her life, and on the other hand the
free community, sovereign over its territory, and actively
building law and institutions from the shared commitment to a common home. If we were to look for a political
document that most perfectly captures this 'European'
vision we should light on the American Constitution, in
which 'we the people' lay down the conditions for our
free coexistence in a place of our own.

This is not to say that there is no such thing as a
European identity. Of course there is such a thing. It
is the identity bestowed on us by that cultural inheritance — an inheritance that is not the exclusive property
of Europe but which is the defining characteristic of
Western civilization in its modern phase. We are right
to treasure this identity, which puts at our disposal the
means of communication with the entire human world.

It is an identity that we share with the Americans, the Australians and the South Americans. It is an identity that is constantly absorbing into itself the cultural and intellectual expressions of other ways of life. And it is an identity that incorporates those universal practices, such as natural science, civil law and tonal music, which speak to human nature everywhere.

This reaching out in a spirit of adventure and enquiry – what Spengler called, in homage to Goethe, the 'Faustian' spirit of our culture – is so striking a feature that people are tempted to believe that the European identity can be understood without reference to its religious roots, that it is nothing *more* than Enlightenment, a purely rational identity that requires nothing of its adepts save an openness and tolerance towards the human world, a *nihil humanum a me alienum puto*, as the Roman playwright Terence expressed it. This is the idea conveyed in the official European documents, which urge us to attach ourselves to Europe while overriding the contours of Europe's spiritual history and its network of inherited obligations. The fact is that we have *won through* to our identity, which is attached to the continent of Europe only because it is there that the struggles and achievements occurred; and it is an identity rooted in the Old Testament and in the Christian vision of neighbour love. It is not an identity that is everywhere shared by

Muslims, whose religion, in its more vehement forms, refuses to admit the legitimacy of secular government or the equality of all subjects, regardless of sex or creed. Of course, Muslims too can adopt a national conception of their public duties, and define their social membership in secular terms. But in doing so they are adopting an identity that is at best only implicit in their faith.

Three and a half centuries of civilization since the Peace of Westphalia have erased many of the linguistic, geographical and cultural boundaries that lay across our continent. It is safe to say, however, that the sense of national identity remains, and maintains its hold over the European psyche. The sense of a pan-European identity is more exalted, more a matter of brain than heart, more aspirational and also, for that very reason, more elusive and fragile. The identity bestowed by territory and self-government is profound and self-evident; that nourished by wider historical, ethical and cultural ties is more tentative and in a way more inspiring. This exalted and fragile European identity is precious. It needs gentle and careful nurturing if it is to grow into something on which we can base our future. To place upon it a vast burden of regulations, in the hope that it will underpin them in the same way that our visceral national sentiments underpin our national laws, is to risk crushing it completely.

In short, if we are to be true to our European identity, this will not be by turning our backs on the nation
state. Nationality is one of Europe's achievements.
The Europeans extracted from the religion of neighbour
love a new kind of sovereignty, and used it to promote
the freedom of the individual under a secular rule of law.
It is on the experience of nationality that the European
Union might have been constructed: a Europe of sovereign nation states, in which powers conferred on the
central institutions could be freely regained from them,
by the same process of negotiation whereby they were
relinquished. That vision, which inspired the foreign policy of Charles de Gaulle, was not accepted by the architects of the EU as we know it. But it is the heart of what
Europe is, as a civilization, a culture and an ideal. And
the British have belonged to that heart throughout their
history, as they can belong to it the more evidently now,
in asserting their sovereign independence.

It is here, however, that we must acknowledge what
is perhaps the greatest problem that our country will
face on leaving the European Union, which is the inevitable confrontation with Germany. I have already suggested that the project of political union has been far
more deeply embedded in the European treaties than
their initial presentation implied. The 'customs union'
was a mask for the pooling of sovereignty envisaged by
Jean Monnet. But beneath even that hidden project lay

another, yet more deeply hidden because it was concealed even from those who pursued it. The Germans
came away from the Second World War with a sense of
their nation as so tainted by things done in its name that
it was no longer possible to identify with it. The national
sentiment that had kept people together through all the
suffering inflicted by the Nazis had to be set aside, an
object of shame and repudiation. Thence arose the impossibility of mourning their losses – the loss of their many
dead, of their fairy-tale towns and cities, of their touching and beautiful homeland and its culture – so that the
wounds of war remained unhealed, and the nation could
not rise again in anything like its previous self-valuing
form. All this is persuasively set out by Alexander and
Margarete Mitscherlich in *Die Unfähigkeit zu trauern* (*The
Impossibility of Mourning*), published in 1975.

For that reason the German people have needed
another way of identifying their first-person plural than
the way of national identity. They have seized on the idea
of Europe as an inclusive project, membership of which
will wash away the sins of nationalism, and include the
German people in a shared and civilized community
of being. To be European is to renounce the old belligerence, the old claims to racial superiority and military dominance. Those things, the Germans believe,
belonged to German *nationalism*, not to us, the German-
speaking citizens of Europe. That old first-person plural

is not ours, any more than the 'we' of Arminius and the pagan tribes is ours.

This collective feeling is largely unconscious and for that very reason hard to escape. The bond between the new Germany and the European project is an *existential* bond. Anything that threatens this bond will therefore be met by a life-and-death struggle. In these circumstances non-belligerence can be a form of belligerence. If your identity, the sense of *who you are*, is bound up with the belief in your gentleness, anyone who questions that belief, or who threatens the conditions on which it depends, must be confronted and disarmed. The understanding of European citizenship, in terms of 'soft power' and inclusiveness, is in Heidegger's terms *existenziell*, not thought out or rationalized but part of *Dasein* itself. The European project has to work, and to work to the full, the Germans believe, if we are to be who we now are. The nation states must not be allowed to abandon us, leaving us with a merely national identity. The British have set an example that threatens us in our very being; they must therefore be punished lest the example be followed.

The Germans are not the only ones with an existential commitment to the European project. 'Ever closer union' is equally necessary, though for different reasons, to the French. Three successive invasions have left a residue of fear that will not disappear just because 'soft power' is written on the face of the one who caused it. Many commentators see this as the explanation for the euro. The common currency, they argue, although long deliberated, and the subject of an enabling commission under Jacques Delors, was hastily advanced by President Mitterrand in a bid to equalize French and German power, following the alarming fact of German reunification. The outside world, witnessing the effect of this project on the Mediterranean economies, might consider it a step towards disintegration. The two principal players perceived it as the opposite. For them it was a move in an existential game, as necessary to soothe the fears of the French as to persuade the Germans that they are more, and not less, European after reassuming their status as the greatest continental power.

The French have not repudiated the national idea. Their post-war stance was one of anti-bourgeois rectitude, together with a purging of the Vichy treason. But the signs are that they are turning towards a recuperation of their cultural heritage. Any hostility towards Britain will stem from another bad example that we are likely to set, over and above that of leaving the European Union, which is the spectacle of a free and lightly regulated economy, and a tax system that encourages the entrepreneurial class to remain settled in the place where they make their money. The statist economy of France can compete more easily with that of Britain, when the same regulations constrain them both. But that is going to change after Brexit. The exodus of the French business class to London will continue, even if it becomes marginally harder to obtain a residence card or to escape the jurisdiction of *les impôts*.

The most important project that lies before us, therefore, is one of conciliation. We must conciliate the Germans and the French in whatever way we can, through cooperative ventures in business, education, culture and foreign policy. How this is to be done in detail is not for me to say. But it should be at the top of the foreign-policy agenda, as vital to the national interest as rebuilding our trade relations with the English-speaking world.

We must also undertake another and equally important work of conciliation at home. We must persuade all our citizens, those who voted to leave the European Union and those who voted to remain, the young and the old, those who live in networks as well as those who are settled in neighbourhoods, the educated and the uneducated, the skilled as well as the unskilled, that they are all part of a single first-person plural, which is to be construed in national terms. We must show that our newly regained independence does not mean turning our backs either on our European allies or on the global economy, that opportunities are as great outside the Union as within it, and that the benefits of leaving will outweigh the costs. To show this will involve radical and comprehensive policies, demanding a shared commitment to belong together, and a reaching out to those for whom voting for Brexit was a visceral response to decades of neglect and humiliation.

Any such work of conciliation will depend on building a flourishing economy, which in turn will need us to leave behind some of the stultifying restrictions of the EU machine. The project of 'ever closer union' was conceived at a time when economic activity was centred on industrial manufacture, and required large-scale capital investment in industries that are inherently volatile and vulnerable to business cycles. The state was often involved in the national economy, either in rescuing key industries from bankruptcy, or in capitalizing industrial ventures that lay beyond the capacity of ordinary investors. Industry was localized in places where raw materials and cheap labour were readily available, and the whole had a character that was both gargantuan and inflexible, with the state and its agencies playing as large a role in stimulating consumption as they played in organizing production. All this is suggested by the project's initial name: the European Coal and Steel Community. And the vestiges of the Keynesian orthodoxies that governed economic thinking in the last days of industrial mass production can be seen today in the state-monitored economy of France.

However, the most vital part of any advanced economy is now the service sector, and the most successful businesses are either information technology companies or 'platform companies', as they have been called, which stick their brand on goods that they would never dream of producing. Firms such as IKEA and Nike are able constantly to expand, while offloading onto their producers (who are often situated in some developing country) the costs of fluctuating demand. As the service economy expands, it is not employment or profits that suffer from economic downturns, but imports. Any cull in the workforce will occur in places that are without real influence over the domestic politics of the countries where their goods are sold. Meanwhile, the service economy grows, displacing the manufacturing sector from the central place that it occupied, until recently, in all government thinking, but which it occupies today only here and there around the world. Some 91 per cent of the American workforce is now employed in the service sector, and even those industries that are engaged in manufacture are beginning to outsource the most volatile parts of their production to places from which they are politically insulated.

Europe's principal capital assets are, in the broad sense, intellectual: its legal instruments, financial institutions, educational traditions and information technology. Devices such as the limited liability company, purpose trusts, the banking system, the stock exchange, insurance, even national currencies, did not come into existence by fiat from some central power. They emerged gradually over centuries: the innovations of Venetian, Genoese and Florentine merchants and bankers, the institution-building genius of Dutch seventeenth-century merchants, the clubbable instincts of the City of London financiers, the foresight of Hanseatic traders, not to speak of the Roman-law concept of corporate personality and the English-law doctrines of contract, equity and trust, all had a part to play in generating the diversified tools of finance and commerce in Europe. Each nation evolved a way of dealing with the complexities of international trade while protecting those who take the risk of it. And in each nation financial, educational and legal institutions became entwined, and connected to the networks and culture of our cities.

The attempt to exert central control over any part of these delicate structures inevitably destroys their most valuable feature, which is their competitiveness. Were the capital assets of Europe vested in infrastructure, engineering works and manufacturing industry, the project of central regulation and control might have seemed sensible, as it was deemed sensible to those who established the European Coal and Steel Community. However, if the European assets were to be counted in those terms, our continent would long ago have ceased to be dominant in the world of commerce. The global economy has moved on since the dreary times of mass production and gargantuan engineering projects celebrated on Soviet banknotes. The future of Europe depends upon our ability to deploy the asset that endows us with our real competitive edge: the intellectual property embodied in our financial, legal, cultural and commercial institutions, in the brains of those who use and learn from them, and in the culture of risk and innovation that has evolved in our major cities.

Thus the institutions that made London into the centre of international finance were not created by edicts from the sovereign power. They were the by-products of business dealings over generations. Their regulations were created from within, by the need for contracting parties to trust one another. And the English law stepped in to make that trust enforceable.

Marx saw capital as possessing a magical, almost spiritual fluidity. It runs to the point where it can be used and finds a route past every obstacle. But his theories do not explain this, since they centre on factory production, in which goods are offered for consumption and value resides (or seemed then to reside) in the labour expended on producing them. The very same image of the factory-based economy was concealed within the original Treaty of Rome, whose 'four freedoms' perpetuate the view of economic value as rooted in the 'factors of production' defined as labour, land and capital. Knowledge, imagination and risk enter the equation, if at all, only because they are implied in labour. But then labour must be understood in its fullest sense, as the activity through which human beings realize their own nature by taking charge of their world. If we are to speak of 'factors of production' therefore, we should acknowledge that intellectual assets are the most important among them, and that knowledge, imagination and innovation are by far the most profitable inputs into any productive investment.

The economic history of modern Europe is the history of intellectual property, which is the commodity that Europe created, the great gift of those Venetian, Genoese and Florentine pioneers, who saw that you could cast this bread on the waters, and that it would return after many days. The moral is therefore simple. We do not sacrifice the advantages of the global economy, nor do we retreat from its cultural side effects, by acting as a nation state, rather than as a member of the European Union. On the contrary the opportunities that lie before us require exactly the kind of flexibility of response that Britain is by nature fitted to exercise, and indeed was first to exercise during the expansion of world trade in the eighteenth and nineteenth centuries. Furthermore, there are old networks of cooperation that our country enjoyed and which were forcibly severed by membership of the EU, notably those built up through the Commonwealth. Whereas much of Europe is in a state of decline relative to the global economy, important Commonwealth countries – notably India, Canada, Australia and New Zealand – are in a state of expansion. All four of those countries look to Britain as a desirable partner and would welcome favourable terms of trade and reciprocal concessions in the matter of work permits and travel visas.

We must acknowledge, however, that the world of intellectual property, virtual assets and invisible exports – this spectral world where our enterprises seem most at home – depends on more earth-bound realities: on the production of goods and services, and more critically on the food economy. Every nation is rooted in the soil and lives off its fruits, and it is indeed a recognition of this fact that motivated the most important and most expensive of the EU's policies: the Common Agricultural Policy, on which all of our farmers have depended for their subsidies. The CAP was initially defended as a scheme with two purposes: to make Europe self-sufficient in food, and to support the small farmer, whose status as a symbol of European peace, stability and beneficence had been the constant theme of wartime propaganda. Self-sufficiency was achieved, largely on account of worldwide improvements in the methods of farming; but the first victim of this was the peasant farmer. Farm subsidies push up the

price, and therefore the rental value, of land, so penal-
izing the small producers who rent their fields, whilst
favouring large landowners and absentee agribusiness.
Hence, while the EU makes payments to over 100,000
different farms and agribusinesses, the top 100 recipients
receive over 23 per cent of the total, whereas the bottom 50 per cent take only 2.6 per cent – which means
that the policy is entirely counter-productive when it
comes to supporting the small farmer. Furthermore, the
CAP has maintained food prices at an artificially high
level throughout Europe, costing the average family an
extra 500 euros a year. It has produced surpluses that
it has dumped on international markets, further alienating food-producing countries elsewhere; and it has
destroyed local food economies across the continent by
imposing finicky standards with which only the supermarket chains and the agribusinesses can easily comply.

France leads a coalition of European member states
passionately attached to the view that rural life requires
protection in a way that could never apply to manufac-
tured goods. This view is by no means a novelty of post-
war European politics. The nineteenth-century British
Corn Laws arose from the same desire to protect indigenous agriculture against imports from America; and the
Corn Laws led to controversies in Victorian England similar to those that surround the CAP today. In the event
the free traders won, the Corn Laws were abolished,

and Britain became dependent, as a result, on imported food – with dire consequences during the Second World War, when the country was on the verge of starvation. Inevitably, in the wake of such a war, a protectionist view of agriculture gains a large number of new subscribers – though not, interestingly enough, in Britain, where the wartime dearth was quickly overcome by importing cheap food from the Commonwealth.

French policy is premised on the additional belief that much of the social capital of the nation is bound up in its rural economy, and that to sacrifice this asset for the benefits of free competition would be to lose sight of the thing that all treaties must ultimately serve, which is the long-term interest of the nation. To the French, and to those member states that look to the French for leadership in this matter, the CAP is a *national* asset, existing to protect the indigenous farmer against 'unfair' competition. The United States, it should be said, is scarcely less protective of its own farm industry, and if the British now think differently in the matter it is not only because the collective memory of the Second World War is fading, but also because fewer people per head of population are employed on the land in Britain than in any other country in the world, save Singapore, which has next to no land in any case.

I dwell on this matter because it illustrates the way in which old and surpassed ways of seeing things are the more easily perpetuated when sovereignty has been removed from the discussion, so that no participant has the ability to say 'we're moving on'. It is of course true that farmers need subsidies, and our government must continue to provide them. But why do they need subsidies? Not because they have no assets of their own. They need subsidies because they cannot realize the value of those assets. A farmer who gains planning permission to build on his land can become a millionaire overnight. We – and we in Britain especially – have prevented farmers from realizing the value of their land, because we regard the land as a public good, not a private possession. The farmer is allowed to own and use his land, but only if he maintains it in the condition that we, the taxpayers, demand. Clearly the whole question of farm subsidies will be clarified and put on a secure and permanent footing once we realize this. We can then reward farmers not according to the size of their farms, but according to the care that they spend on them. The money will not then go to the agribusinesses and the absentee landlords, but to the small farmers who put beauty, wildlife, boundaries, coverts and the local food economy before acreage under plough. An entirely new regime of subsidies, devoted to environmental, aesthetic and recreational goals, would liberate the farmers from the top-down machine, and ensure that the smallest of them get the best deal. Farm subsidies will then be understood for what they are, not payments for exploiting the land, but rewards for maintaining the landscape.

This brings me to the problem that is decisive for the future of our country, and which all recent governments have either avoided or exacerbated: the problem of immigration. Many voters saw the referendum as an opportunity to protest against the vast demographic changes that have been imposed upon the British people without their consent, among which the influx of people from Eastern Europe is only one part. In all matters to do with migration the people have not been consulted, but insulted instead, and the insults were amplified after the Brexit vote. Decades of pusillanimity from the political establishment, and 'virtue signalling' from the liberal elite, have produced a situation in which whole sections of our cities seem to belong to some other country, while housing, healthcare and education are all in crisis from the pressure of incoming numbers. And the cost of this crisis is borne by the indigenous working class, whose assets have been redistributed among foreigners without so much as a by your leave.

In the debates prior to the Brexit referendum, the experts came forward to warn the people of the threatened economic catastrophe, and the Confederation of British Industry (CBI) was prominent among them, telling the voters that the Single Market is indispensable to our prosperity. Many voters, however, were persuaded of only one thing, which is that the Single Market is a benefit to the CBI. When a large business outsources its labour supply to a foreign country, so that its product is brought in from abroad, the local workers lose their jobs. That is bad, but at least the person who has lost his job has no knowledge of the one who has taken it from him. When, however, it is the workforce rather than the product that is imported, and established in the heart of the community whose jobs it has taken, the community suffers an altogether new kind of humiliation.

In the past, manufacturers and service-providers have felt an obligation to offer training and apprenticeship to their workforce, and thereafter to stand in a relation of mutual dependence. Such was part of what Disraeli meant, in advocating the 'feudal principle', namely that the right of property involves a duty towards those who help you to acquire it. However, duties towards the workforce are costly. It is cheaper to import ready-formed workers without assuming any special obligation towards the community in which the business is settled. Ten years ago Britain's largest manufacturing sector – food and drink – employed only British workers. Now one-third of production workers come from Eastern Europe. If the CBI thinks it can persuade the British electorate that this is an overall benefit to our economy, then this shows that its expertise has been purchased at the cost of its intelligence.

Some would like to close our borders completely, others to open them wide. To do the one would be to turn our backs on the global economy; to do the other would be to surrender our home. It is surely time to adopt a clear policy, designed to manage the flow of migrants, not in their interest but in ours. Such a policy does not have to be inhumane. But it has to recognize the constraints on migration that lie in the very nature of the case. A home crowded with people who are not attached to it is no longer a home, and every offer of hospitality to newcomers presumes on the goodwill of those among whom they will settle. There must be terms and conditions, and these must be the object of a nationwide consensus. That consensus will be arrived at only by free and frank discussion, without the name-calling of recent decades. The freedom to travel and to seek employment outside the kingdom is precious to the young, and we must retain that freedom by whatever reciprocal guarantees might be required. But the sense of belonging in an integrated society, in which neighbours are neighbours, and the law applies equally to all, is just as precious, if not more precious, to the rest of us, and can be achieved only by a nationwide effort at consensus. This consensus won't be achieved by censorship and name-calling. It will be necessary to consider both the numbers and the character of those who wish to settle in Britain, and to draw the line with our own national interest in mind.

The right to control borders is the primary expression of sovereignty, and the *sine qua non* of a territorial jurisdiction. Transfer that right to an external body, and the foundations of the state are jeopardized. Yet in all matters arising from the migration crisis the European Union has assumed the right to decide, even proposing a policy of forced settlement on countries that refuse to open their doors. By treating the influx as a European problem, Italy has tried to evade responsibility for repatriating people – largely young men without families – who pose as refugees in order to claim asylum. And by confiscating the problem from its member states, while hiding behind the screen of 'soft power', the EU has made it all but impossible to contemplate the use of force in those places, such as Libya, where the problem originates. At every juncture in the crisis the European authorities have been at a loss, since they have excluded the only factor that can really be applied in seeking a solution, which is national sovereignty. They have adopted a policy that dissolves national borders and the protection that they offer, while erecting no plausible controls over the external border of Europe itself, specifically the Mediterranean shore.

This open-border policy of the European Union is in part responsible for the refugee crisis, since it broadcasts the message that, if you can get to Europe, you will be able to settle anywhere on the continent. Elected governments, which depend upon visibly representing the national interest, can take action to protect their borders, as the Hungarians have done. But the response from the EU has been a series of vitriolic condemnations, and even a move to expel Hungary from the Union altogether. One thing is certain, which is that eruptions of soft-hearted sentiment, of the kind indulged in by Angela Merkel, are, however well intentioned, both illegitimate trespasses on the people who must bear the cost of them, and essentially destabilizing in their effect on social cohesion. Moreover, they cannot conceivably provide a solution to the refugee crisis, since they merely remove from the conflict that causes the problem the people who are needed to solve it: the people who are clever enough, or well-connected enough, to get away, and who carry with them the social capital needed by those they leave behind. As Alexander Betts and Paul Collier have argued in a powerful book, the solution to the refugee crisis is to be found in the havens where the refugees first arrive, and where we can deploy social and economic capital to their greatest advantage, while working towards the diplomatic and military solutions that will enable them to go back home.[2] A policy founded on national sentiment and defence of our borders would encourage this kind

---

[2] Alexander Betts and Paul Collier, *Refuge: Transforming a Broken Refugee System*, London, 2017.

of move, and prove to be much more to the advantage of refugees than encouraging them to emigrate far from home into a way of life that cannot easily include them.

And here it is necessary to take account of the greatest problem that Europe now encounters, the problem of radical Islam. It is a problem that illustrates all that I have written concerning the priority of national identity in any creative thinking about the future. Radical Islamists regard law as stemming from God, and all true obedience as owing to Him. Their thinking is governed by a document that they do not allow to be questioned or critically examined, and yet which contains passages that are incompatible, as they stand, with democratic and secular government and which also are interpreted as a call to war. Recent governments have searched for a strategy whereby to introduce the idea of citizenship to the Muslim community, and to encourage the privatization of the faith. Unfortunately, however successful this strategy may be with immigrants eager for acceptance and work in the host community, it does not prevent the radicalization of their children who, acquiring no national attachment through their school or their largely immigrant neighbourhoods, are apt to turn to Islam in the 'pure' form advocated by the Wahhabist imams of our Saudi-funded mosques. They are seeking not belief but *identity*, the ability to say 'we', without accepting the 'we' of the surrounding culture.

No policy will solve this problem that is not based on a firm belief in the nation and its institutions. Only this will impress on the radicalized youth that there is a real alternative to the violent path that tempts them. The nation state offers the only feasible identity to the young people who have been travelling to fight side by side with their murderous co-religionists in Syria. Meanwhile, we have to school ourselves to live with the consequences of immigration policies that have been not only unwise in themselves, but motivated largely by the oikophobia that I described in Chapter Four. The least we can hope for is that, in the coming years, our governments will put national identity first, and no longer impose on ordinary people the costs of the ostentatious appeasement of their leaders. As for the jihadists in our midst (23,000 according to a recent report in *The Times*)[3] the government will have to acknowledge that the strategy of Prevent is insufficient. Those who travel abroad to fight with the jihadists must be either prevented from returning or put on trial for treason if they do so. A radical policy of internment and deprivation of citizenship will, in the end, be necessary, and we should be thinking of it now.

The perceived weakness of official policy has led to a growing demand from Muslim communities to be governed by shari'ah law – a demand that involves a rejection

[3] *The Times*, 27 May 2017.

of the territorial jurisdiction. Our failure to develop a coherent response to this demand is in part a result of our rooted belief in individual freedom. The French and Belgians have emphatically forbidden shari'ah courts, and the European Court of Human Rights has made no objection to this. We, by contrast, assume that people have a right to 'do their own thing'. So why not a right to the shari'ah? Jurisdiction by confession rather than by territory (the *millet* system) was the Ottoman solution to religious rivalries: so what is wrong with adopting that solution here?

The history of the Middle East is a sufficient answer. Instability there is directly connected with the failure of territorial jurisdiction to take root. Nor is the shari'ah a cogent substitute, since it does not offer to other faiths the space that it claims for itself. Non-believers are at best *dhimmi*, protected by treaty on terms that they cannot negotiate. The result of allowing a group of British subjects to govern themselves according to a religious law would be legalized apartheid, and the destruction of the two most important principles underlying our law: that law is the law of the land, and that it applies to everyone who resides here. These principles have not been simply assumed by the British. They have been fought for. The conflict between Henry II and Archbishop Becket was caused by the latter's attempt to uphold ecclesiastical jurisdiction for the clergy, so creating parallel systems of law in the kingdom, and escaping the judgements of the secular courts. It has been established since that time that there is only one system of law in this country, that the law is secular, not religious, and that everyone must comply with it.

There should be no difficulty in declaring and upholding that principle, and forbidding exemptions on religious grounds. Muslims have to adapt to the single territorial law, just as other British subjects down the centuries have had to adapt to it. As the evidence from Turkey suggests, this adaptation is both feasible and welcome, especially to women. Note that, while the shari'ah permits a man to have four wives, bigamy remains a crime in English law. The conflict between the two systems is therefore irreconcilable. And this particularly atavistic aspect of the shari'ah expresses a conception of sexual difference and the place of women in society that surely does not belong in our country.

The Islamic conception of sexual difference leads, in certain Muslim communities, to the adoption of the full-face veil in public. It is again part of our legacy of freedom that we permit this, as the French do not. But we should recognize how deeply this practice offends against our settled customs. Ours is a face-to-face society, in which people declare openly who they are and address each other as equals. The systematic privatization of women, the attempt to conceal them as secrets, is in part responsible for the failure of certain Muslim communities to integrate. The children of such communities are presented with an absolute existential divide, between the secret place where women are and where children are nurtured, and the illuminated arena of temptations in the world outside. This can only exacerbate their identity crisis, and fuel their desire to join the dark against the light, the secret home against the open society of strangers, the Islamic *ummah* against the secular state.[4]

It is not only in the Western world that the full-face veil is seen as an offence. It is in many places disapproved of in Islamic societies too, and in particular in those, such as Turkey, Syria and Egypt, that have wished to adapt to modern social conditions and to establish jurisdictions that apply to all subjects, regardless of faith. Places where the full-face veil is *de rigueur* are steadily vanishing from the world as we know it, and those Islamic societies where it is deplored are also places where sexual equality and monogamy are now accepted as the norm.

To show real respect for our Muslim citizens is to hold them to the same standard as we hold ourselves. And to those who seem to reject that standard we should put the vital questions: do you, or do you not, wish to belong to a civilization in which women are in the public arena

---

[4] The root of *ummah* is *umm*, mother.

on equal terms with men? Do you, or do you not, wish to live under a shared rule of law, with those whom you regard as infidels? And what, in any case, does your faith tell you about women and how they should be treated? Those questions should have been asked a long time ago, and our welcome should have depended on the answers. But that is no reason not to ask them now, and respect for our Muslim fellow citizens surely demands that we do so.

There is no doubt that the integration of Muslims is one of the important tasks now facing us. In a striking book Douglas Murray has seen in the European reaction to Muslim immigration the signs of the cultural suicide of our civilization.[5] As I have already indicated in Chapter Four, our immigration policies have been not just influenced but, under recent Labour governments, led by oikophobes, for whom the idea of national privilege is unacceptable. Multiculturalism has been a policy directed against majority values, a deliberate attempt to unsettle the indigenous population and to teach it a lesson for being the thing that it is. But we now have an opportunity to put those small-minded castigations behind us, and to affirm what many voters have indicated that they wish their political leadership to recognize, namely our identity as an integrated people, bound

---

[5] Douglas Murray, *The Strange Death of Europe*, London 2017.

together by neighbourliness in a country that we share. Our strategy must be to promote free and public discussion of Islam and its meaning, to put an end to censorship and the retreat behind the veil, and to bring the jihadists into the open where they can be publicly rejected by the Muslim community. And we must extend protection to Muslims who convert from Islam, which will mean dealing harshly with those who attempt to punish them.

The rise of radical Islam brings us to the crucial issue. In periods of enduring peace, such as the one that we have recently enjoyed, people begin to forget why national sovereignty is necessary. Our problems cease to seem vast and threatening, and the illusion arises that they can be handed over to the experts, who will solve them without disturbing the tranquil rhythm of our lives. This 'peace illusion' is expressly fostered by the European Union, which wishes us to believe that peace is the result of bureaucratic government, and not that the bureaucracy came about because at last there was peace. The EU speaks of the 'soft power' with which it approaches every crisis, and extols the virtues of a regime in which diplomacy has replaced force as the means of resolving conflict. And this way of seeing things connects directly with the German identity problem that I discussed above.

In fact, however, peace came about in quite another way, not through soft power but through hard power.

It did not require treaties for pooling sovereignty, but treaties for maintaining rival sovereignties in equilibrium. The UN, the GATT (now replaced by the WTO), and their subsidiary agreements have aimed to settle conflicts between sovereign states, by proposing avenues away from violence. And peace in Europe was achieved not by the Treaty of Rome but by the treaty establishing NATO, which requires from its signatories no diminishment of sovereignty, but rather a commitment to assisting each other in response to any attack. NATO deterred the Soviet Union from extending its control over Europe and did so largely because NATO could rely on the national sovereignty and patriotic commitment of its members, notably the United States and Britain.

The point is of special significance now, when the European Union is increasingly ineffective in asserting any kind of coordinated military strength. By hiding behind the NATO alliance, the Germans have long since ceased to prepare themselves for any kind of war. It is a fundamental truth of military strategy, however, that the preparation for war is the only reliable way of avoiding it, and this is a truth that our military commanders and governments have always acknowledged. It is acknowledged elsewhere in Europe too, but only in those countries such as Poland, Estonia and Lithuania that are directly exposed to the Russian threat. Without going into the complexities it is surely already obvious that, in every

crisis, it is not to Europe that we have looked to protect
our interests, but to our own national resources, and to
the Anglo-American alliance that has twice saved us from
conquest by Germany.

The destruction in the Middle East has occurred precisely in those places – Iraq, Syria, Libya, Yemen – where
the national idea is weak or non-existent, and where
people combine through religious, tribal or dynastic
forms of membership. Tony Blair may have been entirely
wrong to enter the war in Iraq. Nevertheless, he could
expect our troops to fight effectively there, just as soon
as they believed themselves to be fighting for their country. Because of this belief they exhibited the courage and
discipline that have always characterized British soldiers,
when called upon in their country's defence. We don't
make a song and dance about this, since making a song
and dance is a denial of the thing we admire. But that
thing exists, and distinguishes the British military forces
in all their deployments.

One of the most important factors, therefore, in
defining our future path is the perceived weakness of the
European Union in military terms. Few of the member
states have been willing to make their agreed contribu-
tion to the NATO alliance, and the Germans have flatly
refused to do so. In negotiating the Minsk agreement
of 2015, Mrs Merkel and Mr Hollande had no credibility, since they spoke from a position that excluded the

possibility of force. President Putin was merely laughing at them, and the agreement that he signed did nothing to prevent either the entrenching of Moscow's position in East Ukraine or the annexation of Crimea. Observing the behaviour of Russia in those places, on the Baltic border, in Swedish and Finnish airspace and in Syria, must surely give cause for alarm, and it is clear that any perceived weakness will be understood by Putin merely as further encouragement to his policy of reconstituting the Russian sphere of control. The EU downplays strategic threats, inducing in its members an attitude of complacency towards the rapidly changing alignment of forces. Outside the EU, however, in the fresh air of military realism, the dreams and illusions will be blown away. And then it will be clear to us that our survival depends on our military readiness and that our armed forces are a fundamental part of what we are.

The inflow of migrant workers from Eastern Europe is not the result only of the abundant supply of them: it is also the consequence of our educational system, which has betrayed the aspirations and the needs of the indigenous working class. Standards in our state schools have plummeted, to the point where we are near the bottom of the OECD's league table, with 17 per cent of school-leavers illiterate and 22 per cent innumerate. And although our universities remain among the best in the world, there has been a catastrophic decline in the vocational and technical education required to produce a skilled and semi-skilled workforce. Polytechnics used to provide that kind of education, but their conversion to universities led to a softening of the curriculum, while schools and colleges of further education have not taken vocational education as seriously as their pupils need. There is a widespread belief among the young that tertiary education means university or nothing, and career aspirations are turned towards the competitive professions rather than the practical vocations. In 1984, 14 per cent of teenagers went to university; now the number is 48 per cent. In 1973 there were 250,000 apprenticeships; today there are only 50,000, partly as a result of the ease with which firms can recruit ready-skilled workers from Europe. One of the most important policy moves, therefore, if we are to do justice to those who most feel the need for an inclusive *demos*, will be to redesign vocational education. We need to institute the equivalent of the American community colleges, which deliver versatile skills at the place where they are needed, and which support the local identities and the little platoons that are the source of undemonstrative patriotism.

Such reforms should be part of a wider attempt to spread the benefits of economic integration to those whose jobs and attachments fix them to a given place, and who have suffered most from the global market. The global economy sucks finance and innovation away from the small and localized industries, and bestows social, intellectual and financial capital on the giants from elsewhere. Local banks and building societies have been absorbed into the nationwide high street banks, or else nationalized and sold off to foreign competitors, as in the notorious case of Bradford and Bingley. The old understanding of local conditions and the needs of small businesses and frugal households has disappeared from the relationship between the bank and its customers, and people at the bottom of the job market have found themselves without help or advice in their times of need. Many poorer households see banks as part of the alien economy from which they are excluded. Amazingly, 1.7 million adults in our country are without a bank account, many of them now reliant on high-cost pay-day loans to tide them over in emergencies.[6] Rectifying the imbalance will therefore involve an attempt not only to revive vocational training but also to re-localize lending.

Indeed, the new start that Brexit confers on us will be the opportunity to fulfil a project that has been embarked on by several recent governments, which is the move towards a decentralized economy, of the kind that existed in the nineteenth century and could exist again. London outperforms the rest of the United Kingdom in productivity by 72 per cent, a higher score

[6] See Citizens Advice Bureau, pamphlet on *Payday Loans*, published March 2016.

even than that attained by Paris over the rest of France
(67 per cent). Resources, investment and people flow
constantly London-wards, and the South East is not
merely crowded to the point of saturation, but also bears
most of the wealth and social capital of the kingdom.
A conscious effort to direct resources northwards, and
to provide for the people of the northern cities the educational and career opportunities that currently exist to
the south of them, would begin to heal one of the most
painful divisions in our country. The creation of regional
mayoralties is one step in the right direction, but there is
also an argument for state involvement in the process, in
order to incentivize the redirection of social and material capital. Infrastructure projects, inner city renewal,
and an active cultural policy tied to the regions would
begin to answer some of the grievances that led to the
Brexit vote. And we should revisit local government as a
whole, with a view to restoring some of the community-
building confidence of the old parish councils and city
wards.[7]

The North–South divide is not the only wound that
needs healing. The town–country divide is just as serious,

---

[7] See the Tractarian Henry Wilberforce's illuminating defence of the parish, as an ideal of
local government answering to both material and spiritual needs, but at the time when he
wrote rendered impotent by the mass migration to the cities: Henry William Wilberforce,
The Parochial System: An Appeal to English Churchmen, 1838, reprinted Memphis, 2012. On
the historical significance and social strength of the parish, see Andrew Rumsey, *Parish: An
Anglican Theology of Place*, London, 2017.

with an increasingly urban and supermarket-centred population falling out of touch with those who live and work in rural areas. Our planning system has inevitably pushed up the price of land, and also made it difficult or impossible to build affordable housing in the country-side, so that young people have to join the exodus to the city. Addressing this problem should be part of a wider policy of environmental protection, allied to a reform of farm subsidies and a carefully structured diversi-fication of the rural economy. We need to bring small businesses into the heart of rural communities, to pro-vide work and apprenticeships to the young; at the same time we should encourage the growth of a local food economy and an awareness among city-dwellers of the nature and origin of the things they eat. The country-side is rich in social networks,[8] and remains precious to the British people, for the reasons given in Chapter Two. Those who maintain it, as both a material resource and a cultural icon, deserve the support and toleration of city dwellers, the left-wing intellectuals included.

None of this is to deny that our country faces problems, many of which will need the committed cooperation of our European allies if they are to be solved. The first is the problem inherent in our history, and resolved, if at all, only partially and on a temporary

[8] For a true, but anecdotal, account of this, see my *News from Somewhere*, London, 2004.

basis: the problem of Scotland. In the triumphant days of imperial expansion the Scots led the way in trade and colonial settlement; in the two world wars their commitment to the Union was absolute, and displayed in acts of patriotic sacrifice that matched in every way those of the English, the Welsh and the Northern Irish. But circumstances changed. Prolonged peace, EU membership and the subjection of both England and Scotland to the imperatives of the European treaties, have loosened the historical ties, while the creation of a Scottish Parliament, and the consequent conferral on the Scots of a dual sovereignty, has raised the question of Scottish independence in a new form. The toxic mixture of romanticism and resentment brewed by Nicola Sturgeon and distributed free of charge to the people has pushed the Scots to the brink of separation. It would be simple to say: let them depart, and of course we may one day have to say that. After all, it would be of manifest benefit to the English to enjoy a Parliament of their own, in which the opposition is loyal to the same *demos* as the government, rather than the Parliament that we have, in which many of the leading opposition members do not really approve of being there, and do their utmost to penalize the English members for the fault of being there too.

However, we must recognize that the Scottish National Party does not represent all Scots, that the romantic illusions in its leader's head would never survive the social and economic reality of independence, and that the defence of the realm would be seriously compromised by the pacifist policies and neutralist aspirations that she has inherited from her socialist past. It is in the interest of both sides to stay united, and the case for this must be vigorously made, not by politicians only but by those with a voice that is widely listened to. England and Scotland are as closely bound together as Burgundy and Provence; to split apart would not be a liberation but a bereavement for both of them. There must be a serious effort to shift the centre of gravity of our kingdom northwards, to endow Scottish institutions and initiatives with symbolic and ceremonial importance, and even to transfer some of the administration of the kingdom to Edinburgh and Glasgow. The school history curriculum should treat our two countries as mutually dependent neighbours, who face the world together and whose destinies are ultimately one. This shift of the centre of gravity would be eminently feasible, were it not for a singular result of the ill-thought-out creation of a Scottish Parliament, namely, that the English have no assembly of their own. Only if this anomaly is rectified, through the creation of an English Parliament, whether or not housed within the same walls as the existing Parliament of the Union, will it be possible to address the Scots as equal partners in what is, in the end, an ongoing historic compromise, and in no way a form of imperial control.

Taking control of our borders and reducing immigration to manageable proportions will enable us to tackle another of our major problems, which is the housing shortage. Planning is, for many British people, at the top of their political agenda, the one issue that brings them out in mass defiance and causes them to lobby and protest on behalf of what they fear to lose. This fact confirms my thesis in this book, namely that the British identify themselves in terms of the home that they share. Hence they are indignant when that home is desecrated by inhuman architecture or developed without regard for its beauty. These visceral feelings profoundly influenced our pre-war and post-war planning legislation and led to the creation of the green belts, the forbidding of ribbon development and the strict control of building in the countryside. The British people fear to lose what those sensible provisions have until now protected, and we have an opportunity to put that fear to rest, by adopting a new and democratic planning process in which it is not the developers or the architects but the neighbours who decide how a development will look. Instead of the dislocated spread of housing estates without form or character we must try to build the thing that the British people value most, which is *place*. New developments should have streets, squares, shops, schools and public areas, built in sympathetic materials according to local custom and design. And local people should have a say in choosing not just the location but also the look of every building that cuts across their view.

Planning is one of many areas that we can now take back completely into democratic control, in a spirit of national renewal. Another is environmental policy, too long subject to partisan lobbying from groups obsessed with climate change at the expense of all other environmental issues. To free ourselves from the EU's outdated approach to energy solutions, and to look at the environmental question in its totality, so as to enter wildlife, natural beauty and the human habitat into the equation, is one of the greatest benefits that we can hope for from Brexit. It is of course true that environmental problems do not respect national boundaries, and that international cooperation is needed to address the worst of them. And this has been one reason why environmentalists have favoured European initiatives, which are designed to protect the continent as a whole, rather than some arbitrary part of it. But environmental problems are no respecters of continents either, and the record of international climate treaties is dismal in the extreme. Carbon-trading agreements are evaded by the stronger powers, impose unacceptable costs on the weaker, and advance no nearer to the real solution, which is the discovery of cheap sources of renewable energy. And that will require international cooperation of quite another kind.

In *Green Philosophy* (2009) I argued that the root from which all environmental solutions spring is the accountability that binds us to our neighbours. We don't need governments or bureaucracies to implant this motive in us, nor do we need additional incentives in order to act on it. It suffices that we are judged for what we do, and that what we do can be harmful or offensive to others. The point was fundamental to the environmental philosophy of Hans Jonas (*Das Prinzip Verantwortung*, 1979), and also to a long tradition of moral philosophy beginning in the eighteenth century with the second *Critique* of Kant.

Accountability is an identity-forming aspect of the human condition: it is not a matter of what we want, but of what we are. It grows in a specific place, and embraces the people, customs and culture to which those living in that place are attached. Such assets are not to be weighed in the balance and acted on only if the desire to do so is stronger than some competing appetite. They are non-negotiable demands. The desire to protect the environment therefore arises spontaneously in people, just as soon as they recognize their accountability to others for what they are and do, and just as soon as they identify some place as 'ours'. Oikophilia is deep in all of us, and it is illustrated by the ongoing campaign in Britain to preserve the countryside, by the similar campaign in the United States to protect the unspoiled wilderness, and by all the small-scale local arrangements studied by Elinor Ostrom, in a celebrated proof that the 'tragedy of the commons' can be overcome at the local level, when people are conscious of sharing a place as their home.[9] But because this topic is a vast one, and because my response to it has been published elsewhere, I leave readers to reflect on real-life examples. They might recall what happened to the well-managed offshore fisheries of our country, when the European Union took charge of them, or what happened to the American cities when zoning laws and government-imposed freeways tore them apart. It is precisely when decisions are lifted free of the communities that are most directly affected by them that the environmental catastrophe begins. While it is true that we shall always need international cooperation in this matter, it will be worthless if it is not combined with real stewardship over the place that is ours.

Our leaving the European Union does not mean that we are leaving Europe. It is we, the nation states, who have adopted and refined the practice of accountable citizenship, who have established our borders and embellished our national homes with cities, institutions, laws and landscapes that gather our people around a shared sense of belonging. And that represents the true European ideal. We in Britain are not without our

---

[9] Elinor Ostrom, *Governing the Commons*, Cambridge, 1990.

problems; we suffer from tensions of class and ethnicity that often threaten to divide our loyalties; we have suffered from spiritual and cultural decline as a result of losing our religion. But those problems are problems for all communities in the contemporary world, and do not erase the greatest asset that we have, which is our civil society. The British people remain bound to each other by ties of mutual responsibility and social trust, and these bonds have been strengthened by recent troubles. For our ties are not the creation of shallow agreements or passing whims; they belong to our way of being, in the place where we are.

INDEX

INDEX

A NOTE ON THE AUTHOR

SIR ROGER SCRUTON is a writer and philosopher who lives in Wiltshire. He is the author of 50 books, including works of philosophy, history, fiction and criticism. Bloomsbury publishes his classic *England: An Elegy*, the more recent *Fools, Frauds and Firebrands* and *How to be a Conservative*, as well as the *The Disappeared*, a chilling tale of kidnap, rape and trafficking. Sir Roger is a Fellow of the Royal Society of Literature, a Fellow of the British Academy and an Honorary Bencher of the Inner Temple. He currently teaches an MA course in philosophy for the University of Buckingham.

A NOTE ON THE TYPE

The text of this book is set in Perpetua. This typeface is an adaptation of a style of letter that had been popularised for monumental work in stone by Eric Gill. Large scale drawings by Gill were given to Charles Malin, a Parisian punch-cutter, and his hand-cut punches were the basis for the font issued by Monotype. First used in a private translation called 'The Passion of Perpetua and Felicity', the italic was originally called Felicity.